some day soon

some day soon

Essays on
Canadian Songwriters

DOUGLAS FETHERLING

Quarry Press

Some Day Soon is a serious critical study of popular music and Canadian culture focusing on the work of five exemplary songwriters. The quotation of lyrics from the songs composed by these writers is intended to illustrate or explicate the critical argument presented by the author of *Some Day Soon* and thus constitutes fair use under existing copyright conventions. Nevertheless, every effort has been made to notify the publishers of these songs that the lyrics have been quoted by the author. For assistance in doing so, we wish to thank Electra/Asylum Records (Los Angeles); Warner Brothers Records (Nashville); United Artist Records (Los Angeles); Columbia Records (New York); Capitol Records (New York); and Geffen Records (Los Angeles). For bibliographic assistance we also wish to thank PROCAN, CAPAC, SOCAN, and ASCAP.

Photo credits: p. 13: EMP Limited, Toronto; p. 19: National Archives of Canada; p. 23: Reprise Records; p. 27: CBC; p. 31: CBC; p. 37: National Archives of Canada; p. 43: National Archives of Canada; p. 49: Canadian Press File; p. 53: CBC; p. 61: National Archives of Canada; p. 69: Rolling Stone Records; p. 77: Rolling Stone Records; p. 85: Rolling Stone Records; p. 91: United Artists Corporation; p. 99: United Artists Corporation; p. 107: United Artists Corporation; p. 115: United Artists Corporation; p. 123: Canadian Press File; p. 127: American Press File; p. 129: Warner Bros. – Seven Arts Records Inc.; p. 133: Rolling Stone Records; p. 137: Canadian Press File; p. 141: United Artists Corporation; p. 149: Columbia Records; p. 153: Asylum Records; p. 159: Capitol Records, Inc.; p. 167: Reprise Records – Warner Bros. Records Inc.

The publisher thanks The Canada Council and the Ontario Arts Council for assistance in publishing this book.

Canadian Cataloguing in Publication Data

Fetherling, Douglas, 1949-
    Some day soon: essays on Canadian songwriters

Includes discographies.
ISBN 1-55082-000-1

    1. Musicians — Canada — Biography. 2. Rock musicians — Canada — Biography.
3. Popular music — Canada — History and criticism. I. Title.

ML400.F48 1991   782.42164'092'2   C90-090424-0

Design by Keith Abraham. Type imaging by ECW Type & Art, Oakville, Ontario. Printed in Canada by Hignell Printing, Winnipeg, Manitoba.

Published by Quarry Press, P.O. Box 1061, Kingston, Ontario K7L 4Y5 and P.O. Box 348, Clayton, New York 13624.

CONTENTS

For Robert Fulford

PREFACE

Laura Nyro's name is the answer to a trivia question that no one ever asks. To the generation of readers to whom this little book is addressed, however, it just might be familiar. She once had a considerable following as a singer-songwriter, to use the term for a type of performer who became socially as well as culturally important in the 1960s; she came to prominence in 1964, during the folk music revival, when Peter, Paul and Mary recorded her song *"And When I Die."* She was only seventeen at the time, and she easily made the transition to the rock era that followed, prospering artistically and otherwise. She occurs to me now because of a story that used to be told in the record business.

It seems that in some ways she was not very articulate about her music, and it is reported that she went into a studio to record and found herself unable to explain to the sidemen exactly what sort of backup she wanted. All she could do was to tell them to play something that sounded "orange" or else something that sounded "green." One imagines grizzled session hands (who almost certainly had never heard of John Addington Symonds' book *The Key of Blue and Other Prose Essays*) looking about with pathetic expressions and then, somehow, muddling through. It is a fact seldom remarked on, but had Nyro spoken of countries as she did of colours, there would have been less difficulty. Old studio musicians might have known what was required if someone in those days had told them to sound "Canadian." In a metaphorical sense at least, there was a distinctive Canadian sound in contemporary music, though most people were unaware of its singularity. Some of the personalities and attitudes that contributed to this elusive Canadian sound are the subject of what follows.

This is not, heaven forbid, a book about show business, but only a sequence of five essays in what might be called Canadian cultural archaeology, though that phrase is far too dignified for what it describes. The figures whose music and the texture of whose careers I have tried to describe are Gordon Lightfoot, Leonard Cohen, Joni Mitchell, Robbie Robertson, and Neil Young. Biologically, they are of a certain generation (Cohen, the oldest, was born in 1934; Young, the youngest, in 1945). They are all Canadian, though they vary widely in background and geography, and they are alike in having had their greatest success in the United States while managing, each in his or her own way, to keep alive some degree of conscious Canadianism in their work, or at least draw on their Canadian experience. All five came to notice in the 1960s through the agency of personal folk music, though that is as far as one can safely generalize, given the vast musical distance between Cohen's song-poems at the one extreme of complexity and Mitchell's jazz at the other. However little they shared in that respect, they nonetheless weaved in and out of one another's professional lives. And although they are still writing and recording, they seem to us now figures of the 1970s, or so I have tried to picture them here, believing that this period reveals them at their top form as well as at their most characteristic — and at their "most Canadian."

Questions about Canadianness in the performing arts are common but the answers are always vague at best ("If you had dancers from many different countries in a line doing the same move, you could tell the Canadians," Karen Kain has said). They came up during the era discussed here in accusations, for instance, that Joni Mitchell's later music was Californian whereas her first albums were Canadian. They recurred frequently in discussions of other figures such as David Clayton-Thomas who would lend their talents to groups from whom they received as much influence as they gave. To one degree or another, such questions always mask political intent. The month in which I write this, debate percolates in *This Magazine*, the left-wing journal, about whether k.d. lang, whose claim "to be the reincarnation of [the] American country star Patsy Cline is well known" (*ergo*, her band, the reclines), is an appropriate model of Canadian success, given her free-trade alto.

Country music, of course, poses special problems, since it is an organic outgrowth of a peculiar American experience, yet has a resilient Canadian strain based more on class identification than national allegiance. This fact was brought home rather boldly in *Singin' about Us* by Bob Davis, a Canadian songbook published in 1976, at the height of the period discussed in the following pages, that still has relevance for the way it addressed the dilemma. The anthology represented seventeen songwriters, all resident in Canada. They ranged in public acceptance from Lightfoot at the top, through cult artists such as Stringband, topical writers such as Willie Dunn and the Brothers-in-Law, down to the singular case of Stompin' Tom Connors, who was soon to begin a decade-long silence, as a protest, he claimed, against the way Canadian musicians were treated in their own country. Geographically, too, the range was wide. The music itself, however, was defined by politics, so that the book included only country songs or the most nearly c&w work of people not normally associated with that genre. All country music, even that produced by the Japanese, is by its nature American, and yet the editor felt that in this case the "working people [who] are the real heroes of this country" have a proprietary interest in it. And so they do. But that said, he chose only songs whose lyrics included Canadian cultural references or place names, as though these alone made the music Canadian at all or more Canadian than it would be without them. One is reminded of that federal government initiative of the 1940s, as described by Pierre Berton in his book *Hollywood's Canada*, in which Ottawa agreed not to put tariffs on Hollywood movies if the producers would sprinkle the scripts with a few Canadian references, which were assumed to have a salubrious effect on Canada's tourism industry. Berton cites the splendid example of Jimmy Stewart looking heavenward in some forgettable western and for no apparent reason saying, "Those are red-wing orioles from Canada." A non-existent species, an imaginary country.

More to the point, country music depends for its success on an ability to resist change at the proper speed. Lest it put off its conservative audience, it was slow to rid itself of the odd fiddle tunings that dominated from Jimmy Rodgers' time through Hank Williams', and it was with some reluctance that it added, first, the Floyd Cramer piano style, then the pop melodic hook, and finally the rhythm, bass, and drums of rock. Country music adopted Nashville glitter just as Broadway glitter was everywhere being rejected. Throughout its history, country has carefully retained a grass-roots base while at the same time taking on elements discarded by each more progressive wave of music. Canada has certainly had its share of significant country artists, whom the Americans, typically, have thought should feel honoured to be considered as failed Americans. But unlike the five subjects of these essays, they have not, except by the silly place-name test, contributed much that was recognizably different and Canadian. The two words must go together, if one is to judge by the elusive Canadian sound that seems to have existed during the period discussed here.

One of the telling aspects of this Canadian sound was that it developed without much contact with Blacks, usually not even second-hand contact. Another is that its excesses tend to be ones of abstraction and introspection rather than of bluntness. In few of the other arts in English-speaking Canada is the identity crisis made not only a problem but a tradition, and thus part of its own solution. Homer Hogan, an anthologist, hit upon this when, in his song-and-poetry collection *Listen!* (1972), he spoke of Gordon Lightfoot and "the balance of sincerity and restraint in his lyrics and music" — to which should be added, his voice. There is a gentleness in this Canadian sound but a sincere gentleness, not the mock beatitude of the deliberately mellow; it is nervous but not manic. The sound gets its flavour when it combines with a sense of isolation that reflects, even better than most other kinds of Canadian writing, the loneliness of the landscape. If there is one telltale auditory image in Canadian music, it is the grace and dominance of the Prairies carried over into other regions. This image comes across in the way simple acoustics are pitted against complicated vocal progressions. When it works, it works well, and gets under the skin of the geography, though it usually seems to be an accidental occurrence.

There is also a sense of polite, distracted anguish in Canadian song-writing of the period. It is as though the musicians are squinting to make themselves heard or to hear themselves, as though they have taken too many antihistamines, with the result that they seem on the verge of epiphanies which end up as so many depressive daydreams. Or such at least is a quality common in the most representative work of the major figures. In some this anguish overtakes the lyrics, in others the music. In the best-crafted work of the five discussed here it comes out in both to produce a singular effect, one naturally copied by others.

Surely, much of their Canadianness came not from the fact that these five singer-songwriters sometimes mentioned Canada but from the way that Canadian audiences reacted to them differently than foreign audiences did: although I might seem to dwell on their stray Canadian images, it is only to show how they appeared to people listening from this side of the border. Their Canadianness was passive, not active, but it was also therefore a communal activity, and it seems to me that this is a quite important point. As one thinks about these five figures, one sees clearly how important the struggle is between individualism and group achievement in this Canadian context. Lightfoot and Cohen are both, in their different ways, musical loners who have had to confront the group imperative in order to stimulate their careers. Mitchell began as a solo performer but fell into group efforts once she was in the United States; the argument could be made that her alternating periods of pop and jazz are a continued attempt to resolve the conflicting needs to be both a star and to be subsumed into a group. Robertson was a band musician from the start, and although a great future was predicted for him as a solo artist once the band called the Band came to the end of its life cycle, the results have been disappointing, as though the thought of reinventing himself as the primary number had induced some type of creative paralysis. Young has been a congenital player in groups who has pursued a parallel existence as a solo act and encouraged others to do the same. Arranged in this order, the subjects begin to form a progression.

Another fact they hold in common is that all of them have been inclined at one time or another less to the AM hit than to what, until Mitchell and others hit their strides in the early 1970s, was derisively called the album song: the unevenly structured six-minute emotional wonder that did not seem compatible with commercial airplay. When done a certain way, it *sounds* Canadian to ears of a certain age, at least to other Canadian ears, though when done by someone of another nationality it retains at least some of the same feeling. A truly sensitive listener, for instance, should be able to feel if not articulate the Canadianness of Judy Collins' rendition of "*Some Day Soon,*" a tune rich in implication and intellectualized emptiness, even though it is not immediately recognizable as an Ian Tyson song and all the place names are American.

The choice of that example is not without guile. I find it instructive to compare the song with another one of the same title. Shirley Eikhard sang it on the soundtrack of a 1977 Hollywood film entitled *The Domino Principle,* based on a novel by Adam Kennedy. The film was to have made her a star in America as it fulfilled the larger function of revitalizing the moviemaking career of Stanley Kramer. Alas. There was once a special Canadian number of *The National Lampoon,* which featured a proposed new coat of arms for the country. There was a beaver in a Mountie hat rampant on a maple leaf, clutching a sheaf of lightning bolts. Around the top ran the motto SOMEDAY SOON, and around the bottom, MAYBE. Anyone who writes about Canadian culture knows the feeling.

For their help with this project I am indebted to Matthew Clark for sharing his technical knowledge and Vera Frenkel for sharing her reminiscences, as well as to Paul Stuewe for his discographies. Some of the material in this book has appeared previously, in somewhat different form, in *Saturday Night* and *The Whig-Standard Magazine.*

one

GORDON LIGHTFOOT
An Artist of Mood

"Lightfoot is almost as important for what he represents as for what he does."

Gordon Lightfoot is over fifty now, a fact calculated to remind us how time flies and also how little his music has altered over the decades. A critic in *Crawdaddy* magazine some years ago, reviewing GORD'S GOLD, an anthology of redone Lightfoot hits, seemed astounded that "aside from a few slight changes in production, the songs sound exactly the same as they did when Lightfoot originally produced them." The differences may have been slightly more pronounced than that suggests, but they were certainly a long while in coming. Even the obvious shift in his vocal style took place only gradually, or seemed to. The sense of slow motion comes from his unvarying attitudes, the way he keeps returning again and again to a few subjects, and the consistency of his technique: in short, his single-mindedness.

Lightfoot knows what his audience (also over fifty-years old) wants, for he's much the same type as many of them. For commercial purposes he presupposes that they listen to few others with any greater attention than they do to him. He can nudge them along a bit, adding subtle flourishes, pushing back their tastes and prejudices a millimetre at a time. So long as he doesn't rush them into changing, but lets them grow old at the same rate as himself, he is likely to go on forever. When he keeps within those boundaries, nothing can hurt his invisible profile, not even the facts of his early career, which would be an embarrassment to a different sort of star, the kind whose image is based on build-up or slow disclosure, not laissez-faire honesty.

At first glance, his background, like his music, seems, in a word, healthy, and, in another, predictable. He was born in Orillia, Ontario, the Mariposa of Stephen Leacock's *Sunshine Sketches*. His father, also named Gordon, left a nearby farm during the Depression to settle there and married a descendant of the first white child born in the township. The elder Lightfoot worked in a dry-cleaning plant and rose to be manager of it, a position he had held for over thirty years at his death in 1974. His son has never tried to hide the fact that he is a nice middle-class kid, something pop music figures of his generation were not supposed to be. In Canada, at least, he could not disguise the facts anyway since his apprenticeship was so public.

Except for a brief period right after high school when he worked in Toronto as (what else?) a bank teller, Lightfoot has done little but make music. He was a boy soprano in a church choir and got singled out as a soloist for oratorios. He sang in barbershop quartets and won music competitions sponsored by the Kiwanis. In high school he taught himself drums, which he gave up years ago, and got to Grade 8 piano, but didn't begin playing keyboard on records until the mid-1970s. For three years beginning in 1958, when he completed a year of ear training and composition at the Westlake School of Modern Music in Los Angeles, he made two hundred and fifty appearances as a singer and chorus-member on *Country Hoedown*, the hokey CBC television program. He then went to England where he was the host of one called *Country and Western*, by all accounts an unconscious imitation of Canadian imitations of American country-music shows. British television was perhaps even further behind than American television (concerned just then with such controversially denatured series as *Hootenany*) in coming to terms with the fact that they were suddenly in the age of Bob Dylan. It was an epoch in which, in a curious way and for a surprisingly long time, Lightfoot appeared to be an important member.

Before going to England he had done time as a coffee-house folksinger, but on arriving he must have been amazed, as many North Americans were, by the size and resiliency of the British folk scene, with its loyal purists and dedicated hangers-on gathered above pubs like scheming insurrectionists. He must have found in the role of the folksinger a sense of belonging to a generation of musicians. This atmosphere must have given him the desire to do more and better writing. In any event, in 1963 he seems to have thought of himself as a genuine folksinger, but adapted quickly when Dylan suddenly created by example a wholly new kind of figure. Dylan showed that it was no longer necessary to be a pretty singer to be an important one, that you didn't have to be sinatraized. What one had to be instead was, for starters, a combination singer, songwriter, and musician. On a more abstract level, one also had to be a mock-poet and a mock-visionary, even a recorder of personal minutiae. Lightfoot was by no means slow to see that an important shift was underway; but he didn't remain in the vanguard for long.

In 1965, for example, his repertoire included his own early hits such as "*Early Mornin' Rain*" and "*For Lovin' Me*," though he was also singing many folk songs and folk-like songs, including such shop-worn goods as "*Wayfaring Stranger*," "*Foggy, Foggy Dew*," "*If I Had a Hammer*," "*500 Miles*," and, in a nod to Canada, "*Squid-Jiggin' Ground*." By then he'd also incorporated into his act such early Dylan songs as "*Girl From the North Country*," "*Hollis Brown*," "*Blowin' in the Wind*," and "*Talking World War III*," though Dylan himself had moved on to more serious music. While others followed him or tried to, Lightfoot remained surprisingly true to his first set of intentions and as a result came to seem increasingly remote from the mainstream.

If Lightfoot and Dylan weren't peers, at least they were contemporaries.

However mistaken the impression, Lightfoot's career has sometimes seemed to lag behind those of performers with more pizazz, though perhaps that's because he has remained relatively true to his original design. He played the coffee-house circuit of the period, running through a thick gazetteer of places such as the Odyssey in Boston, Mother Blues in Chicago, the Second Fret in Philadelphia. Most especially, though, he played the Toronto circuit along Yorkville Avenue, Cumberland Street, and Avenue Road: El Matador, the New Gate of Cleve, the Riverboat (one that survived until comparatively modern times), the Penny Farthing, and the Purple Onion. He appeared most frequently perhaps at the Village Corner, a small club in a renovated Victorian house at Avenue Road and Pears Avenue. In 1961, in the period between his CBC and his BBC jobs, he was one half of a folk duo called the Two Tones. His partner was Terry Whelan, a local schoolteacher. They cut one album, THE TWO TONES LIVE AT THE VILLAGE CORNER. Its deserved obscurity rests partly in the fact that Lightfoot, discovering it had later been reissued with variations, smashed as many as he could get his hands on with an axe or hammer.

Lightfoot emulated Dylan in important ways. Like many other performers, including some unlikely British ones, he began to sing as much like Dylan as he could. He seemed to exploit the weakness of his voice in the higher register, for instance, just as he would later try to mask it. He affected what sounded like an American accent ("Now the *likker* tasted fine. . . ."). He adopted some of the style the young Dylan had pieced together from Woody Guthrie and other sources. Then as now, he sometimes sang through his teeth, and he tended to end key vocal phrases abruptly and with a sigh. Such borrowings, however, only emphasized the fact that he was writing in the forms Dylan had revived. One early Lightfoot song, "*Silver Cloud Talkin' Blues*," tells how Ronnie Hawkins bought his Rolls-Royce by walking into the Toronto showroom and dumping the cash out of a shopping bag from Honest Ed's, the discount store. But the ways in which he was able to ape Dylan seem less important than those in which he wasn't.

After all, Lightfoot was a Canadian, his phoney red-dirt Okie accent didn't fool anyone, and he didn't have Dylan's powerful outlaw tradition behind him. In the United States the legacy was being used to radical ends in songs which protested even when they weren't strictly speaking protest songs. But among Canadians at this point Buffy Sainte-Marie was the only one to write a notable leftist song, "*Universal Soldier*," and it was careful to mention every conceivable group lest it give offence. (How ironic that by 1989 she would become herself the subject of protests when she began writing songs in support of Major-General Richard Secord, one of the key figures in the Iran-*Contra* scandal during the Reagan administration.)

Although he did write briefly in the protest genre, with songs such as "*Echoes of Heroes*" and "*The Lost Children*," Lightfoot really had nothing to protest against. His distance from the roots of the music he was imitating was such that he couldn't embrace its conservative aspect any more than he could its radical one. Blind adherence to the obsolete notion that the workers were downtrodden good guys was an essential part of American music at the time. Writers were expected to deal with modern themes from a topical perspective, in an attitude and sometimes a vocabulary derived from old blues musicians, vagabonds, losers, Wobblies, and picaresque characters going back to the nineteenth century when rednecks had been reds. Lightfoot found that a difficult assignment. His line in "*Early Mornin' Rain*" — "You can't jump a jet plane / Like you can a freight train" — would have been unthinkable for Dylan, who would have insisted that of course you can, for that's the way to keep the tradition alive. So at the beginning Lightfoot was never quite in sync with his colleagues. Nor did he seem destined to have much lasting importance as a mere performer, though he became a polished one in time. He was, however, a prolific writer, and that was to be the basis of his career.

Lightfoot is a blend of performing artist and recording artist without being either in particular. His personality in concert seems identical with the one on disc. On stage, there is little patter and no tuning up, only slow, even melodies. These performances are highly professional, yet the slickness is hidden by sincerity and lack of adornment. The recordings and the concerts are the way they are, one may hazard, because they are both secondary to the writing. It is in the writing that the natural feeling originates.

Much of Lightfoot's peculiarity is the way he has managed to write so steadily and evenly. Throughout the 1960s and 1970s, no one creative year was markedly better than any other. He paced himself in such a way that his career has been almost wholly free of fits and starts, externally or creatively. Partly this was due to the way his lyrics and melodies balance: almost never is one more striking than the other. His songs, more than almost anyone else's perhaps, are total works in this way. Parsing them is difficult considering how simply constructed they are, but it is probably the best way of understanding how he has played the tortoise in a tortoise-and-hare relationship with contemporary music.

Lightfoot's music has the ability to convert the listener to its mood very quickly. Such speedy atmospherics are the source of his effectiveness; one is always conscious of the feeling one is supposed to feel. For all its ease and melodiousness, however, the music is the opposite of Muzak, depending on the listener's attention to the emotional state currently on the agenda, which then quickly becomes the listener's own. Its ability to dominate gently in a short time is the better part of its utility. No doubt the speed with which the music establishes itself is what some ad executives were thinking of when they once instructed Warren Zevon to write "folksy, Gordon Lightfoot commercials" for television. Because of this instant intimacy, Lightfoot's melodies often give the feeling that you've heard them before even when you haven't, though that is not why Lightfoot ingratiates himself with the audience as a believable old family friend. No,

"Lightfoot's melodies often give the feeling that you've heard them before even when you haven't."

that particular trick has more to do with the lyrics. Appearances to the contrary, Lightfoot would be unthinkable as an instrumentalist.

In a society full of tension and abrasion, Lightfoot's music soothes. In an environment obsessed with information and detail, it seems satisfyingly intangible without ever lacking direction. True, he has written about specific historical events or contemporary happenings ("*Canadian Railroad Trilogy*" and "*The Wreck of the Edmund Fitzgerald*"); such songs have been among his most popular. But they're not typical. Characteristically, he writes about hazy personal relationships whose very impermanence he pinpoints with generalities. He has often done this most effectively when writing in impressionistic rather than factual ways about the Canada he knows. For instance, "*Does Your Mother Know?*" had a meaning for Canadians in the late 1960s that it must have lacked for other people at a later time. It caught the essence of the spot Vancouver held in the imaginations of a particular generation, the one for whom 4th Avenue in Kitsilano will always be associated with a close community of lonely street-people.

Another Lightfoot trait is the way he laments, often unconsciously, a past he was born too late to have experienced. He often expresses the loss in imagery about personal relationships or nature, lumping everything together so that the entire past becomes a single period extending right up to the present moment. The technique makes it natural that in "*Old Dan's Records*," for example, he should write "Dig out Old Dan's records / back to 1935 / the foxtrot, jitterbug and jive," as though these three distinct styles of music were all the same in age and sensibility. These particular lines are unusual, however, in that he normally achieves his conception of the past the same way he achieves his idea of the present, without resorting to references from popular culture. Another exception is the lyric of that haunting song "*If You Could Read My Mind*":

> Just like an old-time movie
> about a ghost from a wishing well
> In a castle dark or a fortress strong
> with chains upon my feet
> You know that ghost is me
> And I will never be set free
> as long as I'm that ghost
> that you can't see.

The old-time movie in question is *The Canterville Ghost*, a 1944 comedy in which Robert Young, an American soldier stationed in Britain, discovers that he is descended from a seventeenth-century ghost, played by Charles Laughton. The ghost is doomed to continue as a disembodied spirit until some member of the family performs an heroic act. The film is of no special importance or distinction or even relevance to the song, but is one Lightfoot doubtless remembered dimly from childhood or the late show. The reference makes an interesting comparison with two lines in Dylan's song *"A Simple Twist of Fate"* — "I still believe she was my twin / but I lost the ring" — which sounds like a reference to *The Prince and the Pauper*, *The Merchant of Venice*, or perhaps *Elizabeth and Essex* but in fact turns out not to be a literary allusion at all.

It sometimes appears that Lightfoot's tradition is his sheer traditionlessness and cultural confusion ("Canadian Rail*road* Trilogy," not Rail*way*). But for all that, he fits snugly into the pattern of Canadian culture by his frequent awareness of this condition, sometimes in songs about the United States. Two albums from 1968, DID SHE MENTION MY NAME? and BACK HERE ON EARTH, contain much of his best work from the period when he was recording with United Artists. Between them they show his full range, from the overtly country to the mellowness he would later explore more deeply when he moved to the Reprise label, a division of Warner Brothers. Each LP also contains songs about some aspect of the United States. "*Cold Hands from New York*" and "*Affair on Eighth Avenue*" show the U.S. as threatening, and "*Black Day in July*," his song about the Detroit race riots of 1967, projects a sense of moral superiority that is probably not misplaced. The song was banished from the playlists, not of the Detroit stations, but of CKLW in Windsor; it is somehow revealing that the only Lightfoot song ever proscribed was banned not for sexual or drug references but for fear of bad manners and by Canadians to whom its sentiments are a conversational commonplace.

DID SHE MENTION MY NAME? also contained "*Boss Man*," a piece in the southern blues tradition from which, as the song shows, he is so far removed that one is almost reminded of W.H. Auden's brief flirtation with "blues" poetry in the 1930s. This too shows the Canadianness of his work, for Canadian music, as distinct from American, developed without much contact with Blacks, usually not even at second hand. "Boss Man" is in a certain musical style without having the necessary sociological roots. Lightfoot on a white background merely sounds white, most often without reference to the nationality; Lightfoot on a Black background sounds squeaky clean. It was no doubt his remoteness from Black-influenced culture rather than merely from Black culture itself that Robert Fulford was alluding to in a crack about Lightfoot's appearance with Dylan and Joan Baez during their Rolling Thunder Review concerts in Toronto in 1975.

He remarked that "up there on stage Lightfoot looked like Frederick Philip Grove trying to elbow in on a conversation between Dostoyevsky and Nabokov."

Later, on his Reprise albums, Lightfoot mentions the U.S. without his previous sense of alienation, and such changes go together with a new attitude towards Canada too. His patriotism has always been *sotto voce*, at least after some early attempts to show the flag turned into embarrassing failures. In 1965, when he was still performing "*Foggy, Foggy Dew*," he was also singing "*Song for Canada*," a tune written by Ian Tyson and Peter Gzowski. For several years after that, any patriotic feelings of beer-commercial intensity lay hidden or found less obvious expression perhaps, as in the melodic bounce of the railway trilogy (which of course is no trilogy at all but a composition in the strict sense, woven from more than one distinct melody line — as in his later and equally ambitious song "*The Patriot's Dream*").

No part of Lightfoot's writing is so important as the whole of it, or so impressive. That's the secret of his longevity. He is unusual among the folk-based singer-songwriters in being a trained composer. If his lyrics, snatched out of context this way and laid out on a printed page, sometimes seem even more lifeless than popular song lyrics generally do in such circumstances, his melodies, isolated the same way, are equally flat, which is more unusual. One of the keys to Lightfoot seems to be that the one component is seldom allowed to overpower the other. He's all of a piece. His style is seemingly to be without style. It is there that his skill (as distinct from his talent) comes into play.

To say the least, he maintains a low melodic profile in his songs. On an oscilloscope, his music would be shown by an endless series of low, gently sloping curves; no sharp peaks, no unexpected dips. The commonly accepted view is that his music is repetitious; one old acquaintance likes to annoy him by remarking of each new song that he liked it better the way it was written last time or the time before that. But on examination he appears to be just maddeningly consistent rather than limited.

He came of age musically when most of the other folksingers operated by dint of creativity, without benefit of theory. They were three-chord writers, with a special fondness for C, F, and G in the key of C. Lightfoot, for all the simplicity of even his most complex songs, has never been one of them. He uses pretty much the entire elementary system of music he learned in Los Angeles. Generally, he plays guitar only in the easy keys, for he likes that open-string sound necessary to the genre. His favourite key is D by an overwhelming margin; within it, he'll use most everything he can find. What flashiness there is on his albums comes from the arrangements and production values, not from the writing, and even such decoration as does present itself became obvious only in the middle 1970s. He doesn't experiment because, as an artist of mood rather than form, he wants as little tension as possible in his music. So his tunes, his harmonies, and his rhythm are more of a total package than those of most writers are. Still, it is necessary to look at them individually to get a sense of how he keeps them together.

There cannot be many major songwriters with Lightfoot's method. Certain chord progressions or bits of melody, perhaps even rhymes, occur

"In a society full of tension and abrasion, Lightfoot's music sooths."

to him from time to time, and he files them away in his head, not on tape or paper. Then, once every year or so, he simply holes up somewhere and writes an album's worth of material all at once. The process usually takes months, but early in his career he wrote an entire LP in four days (like many other songwriters, he often begins with a title; the phrase "carefree highway," for example, popped up on a sign outside Flagstaff, Arizona, and turned out eight months later to be the name of a song on the SUNDOWN album). Once he commences to write songs from the accumulated ideas, however, he sets down melodies on manuscript paper rather than first working them out mentally and then on tape, as most others of his generation do; perhaps this helps explain his consistency, as the printed staff makes for a slower pace and tends to inhibit what seem like brilliant flashes. What's less surprising, though equally important, is that he writes with a guitar in hand, rather than at the piano. That may be a clue as to why his melodies seem written to go with the chords instead of the other way around.

All of which is to say that, though he is prolific, his main attribute is not fecundity but probity. He does not write so much that he has to throw away a lot of it in order to show off the best. His recorded output includes one or two indisputably awful examples of the craft (such as "*Rosanna*," a deadly bit of business, or "*Go Go Round*," a song about a go-go dancer that is mediocrity taken to the point of inducing pain). But there aren't many, because the editing process is almost completed before the writing has begun.

A typical Lightfoot song will hold one note for a long while. When he does move on, he does so in scale passages. He seldom skips, and then usually only to a chord tone. This technique makes for dull songs but smooth ones. His melodic lines contain few surprises, a fact that he only emphasizes on disc and in performance, belabouring the melodic phrases when he sings them. Unlike Dylan or Joni Mitchell, he sings bars of music and multiples of bars, not between bars. Sometimes he will suspend a note atop a chord. He will often use an *appoggiatura*, another note of embellishment. But those are practically his only melodic gingerbread. His songs as written are minimally ornamented. He sings them that way too.

In a curious way, such a songwriting style says something for his being a Canadian because it bespeaks a lack of a clear, recognizable tradition of *recorded* popular music. Dylan, as a writer and as an influence on others, even long after he ceased being a singer of actual folk songs, remained, at least melodically, within the Child tradition of British folk song and its more colourful American variations and permutations. Canada has similar though different traditions, but they are somewhat regionalized; Ontario, for instance, has a fine heritage of indigenous folk music that remains largely unrecorded and so only a very few nationally known figures have been influenced by it (such as Stompin' Tom Connors).

The fact that Lightfoot has only one pedal extremity in the folk tradition is evident in his use of harmony as well as in his melodies, for harmonically he goes out of his way to avoid tension-peaks on the graph lest they destroy the mood. He normally works only in the major scale, going outside only for modal rather than structural reasons. He won't actually enhance his songs, he will only daub them with colour. He'll use a secondary dominant chord if he must, flats and sevenths if he has to. But like most people in the genre he will rarely if ever modulate or go outside the key to make a livelier song.

His favourite way of adding tone colour is to write in the Dorian mode, which was used commonly in English and Appalachian folk music (and in a great deal of what's come later) — *re* to *re* in the major scale (or D to D on the white keys of the piano) instead of *do* to *do*. It is in fact the only mode he uses. An example is "*Pussywillows, Cat-tails*," whose musical feeling reinforces in the lyric by piling gentle, disconnected images on top of one another.

```
Em            D        C           Em
Pussywillows, cat-tails, soft winds and roses.

                        D        C         Em
Rain pools in the woodland, water to my knees.

Am7           D        G           E
Shivering, quivering, the warm breath of spring.

Em            D        C           Em
Pussywillows, cat-tails, soft winds and roses.
```

The song first appears to be in the key of E minor. But if it were, the D chord strictly speaking would not be allowed. He has abandoned the minor key for the Dorian mode. The E major chord, like the D, is there solely for reasons of colour.

Generally, Lightfoot plays about twenty chords on the guitar, an adequate number for a modern popular songwriter, and he gets a remarkable range of effects from them. His chords ordinarily contain only three notes — basic triads. There are two other kinds he could use — ones with notes built on top or extended on alternated chords. The first of these he rarely makes use of, for by doing so he would jolt the listener accustomed to hearing his albums almost as though they were continuous wholes, not collections of individual songs. The second type is one that came into being for melodic reasons and was only later accepted as harmony. A piano player in some early jazz band, for instance, may have added an extra fancy note to relieve the boredom or make his contribution to the number a little more distinct, causing other members to begin playing it as well until, at length, the coinage became harmony instead of merely melody. Typically, he will play them on the guitar without singing them.

Not that the songs are so predictable as all that. Sometimes he'll make use of unusual chords (unusual for him at least), as when he used Dmaj7 in the melody line of *"I'm Not Sayin'"* in order to pep it up a bit, because he felt the need of singing an odd note (C sharp). By contrast, Dylan will play the tonic against the dominant, singing in one key while blowing harmonica in another. But Lightfoot can't do that because he has only himself and his guitar to work with and, in any case, has only a toehold in the folk blues tradition. In *"Rich Man's Spiritual,"* for instance, he writes strictly in accordance with the cycle of fifths — C–A–D–G–C — even though he is writing a blues. He could have put sevenths atop all those chords, utilizing what is called a salty-dog progression. But that would have made the song a rich man's not a poor man's spiritual, a Black song rather than a white; and Lightfoot is very WASP, uninfluenced by the blues tradition beyond the extent to which it is history and the degree to which "blues" and "spiritual" make nice song titles.

His notions of rhythm are naturally in agreement with his ideas about melody and harmony, and are closely tied to his ability to perform songs as part of the process of writing them. He is a simple but effective guitar player, simpler even than, for instance, John Prine, but like Prine carries a nice steady rhythm with a flat pick. The rhythms of his songs are therefore very even. He writes a lot of quarter notes in neat sequence and doesn't syncopate much. All the while he balances his songs carefully so that one part has no heavier a rhythm than the next. That is, he repeats musical phrases, only sometimes adding tags to the second phrase so that the effect is sameness without sterility. He commonly writes in either 3/4 or 4/4 time. By contrast, even Bruce Cockburn, an artist from the same tradition, has written in 5/4 (a signature that the Beatles made respectable in popular music). But as in so many other areas, Dylan provides the clearest comparison. Dylan's harmonic vocabulary isn't any wider than Lightfoot's, but his melodic vocabulary is almost absurdly more extensive. Rhythmically Dylan changed the way people listen to chords, with his delight in a choppy, syncopated style, a style that had immense impact on almost everyone, it sometimes seems, except Lightfoot.

*"No part of Lightfoot's
writing is so important
as the whole of it, or so
impressive."*

In the early United Artist days Lightfoot was content with a solid Canadian reputation, the cross-country tours, his annual Massey Hall concerts, the campus dates, the FM power base highlighted by occasional forays into the U.S. That changed in 1969 when he switched to Reprise. Lenny Waronker, his producer at the new label, would be much more involved in shaping the sound than his previous producers had been, extending the instrumental range of the music with concertina, mandolin, classical guitar, and dobro. Under Waronker, professional arrangers were brought in. Lightfoot himself became more ambitious, adding twelve-string guitar and broken-chord piano to his standard acoustic guitar work. By 1976 the two of them working together could even use a Moog (on SUMMERTIME DREAM).

That was the album that contained "*The Wreck of the Edmund Fitzgerald*," based on news reports of the sinking of a Great Lakes ore carrier in a storm the previous November. Like so much of his work, the song employed only one musical (rather than literary) idea, the repetition of a simple but distinctive four-bar phrase; the lyric, in strict ballad form, with many factual details, fitted round the phrase for twelve stanzas and was sometimes bent into the melody's shape. There was not much Waronker could do to lessen its shortcomings without diminishing its primitive strengths. There, in a nutshell, is the problem with Lightfoot and the secret of his power.

Many other performers have sold more records and tapes than he has (though, at a guess, he's sold maybe fifteen million). Few, however, are likely to sell so much so steadily and evenly and thus become so important in the catalogues. Some writers are more often recorded by other performers, but Lightfoot is an extraordinarily dependable source of material for certain types of artist. And in the first years of his international success he was actually rather astounding in this regard. "*Early Mornin' Rain*" was covered by everyone from Judy Collins down through Johnny Cash to Harry Belafonte and the Kingston Trio, and at one point in 1965 was on three of the fifty topselling LPs. There are more than a hundred versions of "*For Lovin' Me*" and an equal number of "*If You Could Read My Mind.*" Those figures put him in Lennon and McCartney's league as a copyright artist.

A generation ago, when the Canadian Radio-Television and Telecommunications Commission introduced Canadian content rules for radio stations, overnight creating a recording industry of sorts, Lightfoot took an unpopular stand, saying that he would rather "compete with everyone in the music business in general . . . not necessarily with other Canadians." In the present era of free trade, that long-ago remark assumes new relevance. For all the special Canadianness of his music and his attitudes, Lightfoot's position is much the same in Canada as it is in the U.S. It is somehow significant, though, that he and Anne Murray are far and away the most important popular musical figures to have remained so successful for so long without moving away. In an environment in which culture is at times a branch of politics because of the role it plays in the national purpose, Lightfoot is almost as important for what he represents as for what he does. What he represents is, like his music and his career, simple, but deceptively so. Even when his music does not seem at all interesting, the means by which it gives that impression can sometimes be fascinating.

two

LEONARD COHEN
The Sound of Mercy

"Listening to Cohen would have to be like eavesdropping on some famous and tragic figure in the past."

Leonard Cohen, as usual, is making a comeback. First there was *I Am a Hotel*, the video that married his music with Ann Ditchburn's choreography. Then came his guest shot on *Miami Vice*. More recently, but far most importantly, there was FAMOUS BLUE RAINCOAT, the album of his songs by Jennifer Warnes (who used to be Jennifer Warren and one of his back-up singers). That led in turn to the release of I'M YOUR MAN, his first album in years and one of his most successful in every sense. There are even plans for a new Cohen book. Yes, the doleful loner with the zippers on his wrists is emerging from the shadows once again, more or less on schedule.

He's over fifty now. That's old enough so that Suzanne Vega acknowledges in public how Cohen has influenced her music, old enough so that members of Famous Blue Raincoat, a popular Edmonton band, cannot remember when he played a club in their city called the Yardbird Suite. His age also means that he has been writing for more years than Byron, Shelley, Keats, or Rimbaud lived. In that time, his work has changed more than some critics have acknowledged, but it has remained unalterably in the tradition of the young romantics, by turns fiery and long-suffering, nostalgic and messianic — the roses and razor blades school. He belongs to a league whose members customarily write themselves out, commit suicide, or go into business by their early thirties at the very latest. Yet there he sits, or stands, sounding and indeed looking much the same as he ever did. But how? Which is also to say, why? For answers it is perhaps necessary to go back to his beginnings, to when he first arrived, when comebacks were not yet possible, when he was a literary person and not yet known as a musician.

He was doing his freshest and most disciplined writing at a time when other people were putting into song lyrics a great deal of energy that would otherwise have gone into verse, and most of the audience was retooling the same way. He was part of the first generation in modern times to leave open for themselves the option of music — a fact that may very well have saved his creative life. In time, perhaps in the nick of it, Cohen's poems began turning into song lyrics. The transition affected only his metrics, not his basic style, and gave his talent a new vigour. It also provided an audience far larger than even he, a popular poet to begin with, could have imagined.

His songs are made of lush imagery and spare melodies. In Canada their appeal was evident from the start, even before he began recording, and in the United States their renown was simply multiplied by ten. In Europe he was so popular, it was said, that if any young French woman owned but one record, it was likely to be one of his. And such is the slower cultural metabolism there that he stayed popular longer than he did in flighty North America, though fashion is not the only explanation for his enduring appeal in Europe. His music is in the tradition of personal statement that is more common in the home of the art song and *chanson* and predates the enforced egalitarianism of radio. If his music is not precisely Continental, it is certainly not American pop. It falls somewhere between, both musically and lyrically, fed by those two environments but dealing, subliminally, with a third. You could say that, appearances to the contrary, Cohen has remained a Canadian artist at least in that he draws on a part of Canada's literary heritage which, while it has counterparts elsewhere, is still one he knew and participated in for so long.

Cohen was born in Montreal in 1934, and it is important to an understanding of him that he's not just a poet but specifically a Montreal poet. It was not long after they introduced modernist poetry to Canada in the 1920s that the revolutionary English-language Montreal poets began to seem stylistically conservative compared to those of Toronto and later Vancouver. They also tended to be natives or long-time residents of the city, far outnumbered by the French Canadians, and therefore closely knit and less conscious of differences in age except insofar as such differences seemed to encourage mentor-disciple relationships. In his verse and later in his songs, Cohen always has seemed a person struggling to break through some invisible ectoplasmic wall separating him from the majority. His predominant theme, usually dealt with in the most personal terms, has been alienation in the literal sense — the condition of being an alien. At a metaphorical level it has two forms, the alien as outcast and the alien as endangered species. The Leonard Cohen who is the subject of the books and music (a creature who may or may not have much in common with Leonard Cohen the person) is reminiscent of some Graham Greene character one would expect to see at the scene of every retreat from imperial power, every sharp eclipse of old western values. He is forever one step ahead of some great beneficent calamity. A single individual facing the tide of events, Cohen must content himself with love — or at least sex — among the ruins.

His roots, however, are as much in a general bohemian past as a particularly Montreal one. His reputation is either marred or enhanced by the fact that most of his friends and contemporaries have remained in Canada and feel free to discuss the atmosphere they shared with him. Conversation with them usually reveals that the early years of Cohen's creative life were heavily, sometimes self-consciously, patterned on the familiar principles of what might be called landed bohemia. All the elements are there, including the delight in outrageous behaviour and the feeling that it should not disqualify one from respectability, the need to rebel against authority and the equally strong need to conform to the established pattern of such rebellion. He was the issue of a well-off Montreal family and rose up against that fact while at McGill, the customary resting place of such individuals. It all seems so cozy.

It apparently was assumed that on graduation Cohen would enter the family clothing business. But he switched from commercial studies to an arts course and quickly came under the influence of much older Montreal poets both within and without the university, figures such as Louis Dudek, F.R. Scott, and most especially Irving Layton. In the late 1950s, Layton was nearing his peak as a public personality, consistently damned or loudly ignored for his poems of (what then was considered) excessively frank sexuality. He was looked on, mostly with derision, as something of a Canadian beatnik, a judgment shared, though of course without the calumny, by some of the Beats themselves. He was even photographed by Fred W. McDarrah of the *The Village Voice*, the Yousuf Karsh of the anti-establishment. Layton dominated the Montreal scene by his presence and the rest of the country by his bombast. Cohen quickly went into Layton's debt as a poet. But perhaps the greatest lesson he learned from Layton was about the value of a pubic mask.

Cohen received his BA in 1955 from McGill and later did postgraduate work at Columbia, though he remained active in the life of Montreal. In time he became one of the pre-eminent figures of the city's still largely unchronicled English bohemia. Stanley Street, with its Hungarian and Spanish coffee houses and small galleries, became his Stanyon Street but also his boulevard Raspail. Like all bohemias, though, it was given focus not by real estate but by people of similar temperament, vying for status as artists, which only the most ambitious would ever achieve.

One hangout was a coffee house called the Pam-Pam (long since licensed and renovated beyond all recognition), where the writer Stephen Vizinczey worked for a time as a fifteen-dollar-a-week dishwasher. Another was the McGill Union on Sherbrooke Street, now the McCord Museum. Along with his friends, Cohen read poetry to middle-of-the-road jazz in a room above Dunn's Famous Delicatessen and, much later, decorated the Tokai with his presence. Realizing how many of his acquaintances were painters, Cohen and three partners opened the Four Penny Gallery, which lasted until the building was destroyed by fire. The gallery was notable because the proprietors habitually painted all the frames in bright primary colours, thinking to enhance the works therein. "It was very Alexandrian," one survivor from the period maintains. "Everything was treated as theatre."

Such veterans abound. It is not difficult, for instance, to discover people of Cohen's age who are willing to identify by name the Nancy of "*It Seems So Long Ago, Nancy*," or to reveal the true identity of the person who inspired his song "*Suzanne*." (Actually, the best research indicates that there were then three Suzannes in the Stanley Street mob: one a French Canadian who became a dancer, another a Swiss who became a play-wright, the third a woman whose origins were as mysterious as her eventual fate, as befits the possible Dark Lady of Cohen's sonnets.)

The circles he moved in, then, were crowded with people struggling to be talented, many of whom later found careers outside the arts (one of his early friends, for example, was Lionel Tiger, the anthropologist). These friends leave a portrait of Cohen as a sullen, lonely fellow with a slight weight problem. Just as he has done in his music, Cohen made strengths from his weaknesses. Solemnity of a particular sort became his vocation. In keeping with the bohemian spirit of the 1950s, he elevated his personal discomfort to the level of anguish and then used it as a metaphor, and himself as a symbol, for a world whose complacency seemed to be leading to annihilation. From the social he waxed sociological. His writing only served to clarify his public persona rather than reveal what lay beneath it.

In his undergraduate days Cohen started building a reputation as a writer of anti-romantic or dark romanticism, one from which he has seldom deviated. It was only after graduation, however, that he legitimized it in the eyes of his contemporaries, and perhaps his own as well, by publishing a book. Louis Dudek, the main poetic presence on the McGill faculty and a person who could claim personal acquaintance with Ezra Pound, conceived the idea of a series of poetry chapbooks by students. The first title was Cohen's *Let Us Compare Mythologies* in an edition of a few hundred copies. Its appearance in 1956 consolidated Cohen's position in Montreal's tight little arts world and may have influenced his decision to limit his postgraduate stay at Columbia and return to Montreal as a bohemian prince. From that point on, Cohen was marked for a literary career. Although his books were slim and far between (the second, *The Spice-Box of Earth*, didn't appear until 1961), he was able to live off his image for long periods like a bear off its fat, for the persona and the writing were each other's cause and effect.

Cohen's image was that of someone struggling to remain a romantic in the face of harsh realities and only subordinately the beatnik variation of that: trying to remain an individual in the face of governmental and social depersonalization. In 1959 he made his first visit to Greece, drawn there either by its beauty and low cost of living or by the way it had called the romantics of old from whom he seemed descended. For a number of years he made frequent visits, eventually acquiring an unheated mountain cottage on Hydra to which he would retire for long periods. The Grecian part of his life, while it did not provide an obvious backdrop for his writing, became important in his mythos. He alternated between time there and lengthy stays in Montreal; even in interviews given after his recording career began, he always seemed to be just arriving from or just departing for one place or the other.

Reviewers usually took a politely ambiguous position on his poetry, praising him for his versecraft, which was then still conventional, but

"In his under-graduate days Cohen started building a reputa-tion as a writer of anti-romantic or dark romanticism, one from which he has seldom deviated."

sometimes expressing uneasiness about the sensual and sybaritic images upon which the poems depended. Yet he was clearly a comer, and for years, until first Margaret Atwood and then Michael Ondaatje became important, he was the youngest writer included among the more conservative poets, junior division, and for a time it appeared as though he was proceeding towards the standard literary career — living from grant to grant, his progress enlivened by considerable infighting and punctuated by the occasional university appointment, the odd editorship of this or that publication. It was as though he had achieved the true bohemian ideal of respectability generated by disrespect. When, in 1960, he applied for his second bursary from The Canada Council, he did so by driving from Montreal to Ottawa in a hired limousine he could not afford and terrorizing the council staff by chasing them in a motorized wheelchair he didn't require. Such stunts were uncharacteristic, however, for generally he was content to be the tortured soul seeking transcendence.

A quasi-religiosity, which he sought to have interpreted as spirituality, permeated his public space, both on the page and in the flesh. He played the role of the guilty one yearning for atonement. Saintly, if no saint, he cultivated the image of one who has passed from rascality to martyrdom without the intervening stage of devotion. Like Gordon Lightfoot, what he projected most clearly was the vulnerability of the artist, not that of the common man (whereas many of Lightfoot's song titles are questions, many of Cohen's are sad statements).

The almost untenable sadness is what best survived the filter of his personality. In 1961, for instance, the McGill bookstore ordered his new book *The Spice-Box of Earth*. The clerk who unpacked them was startled to find that the copies were blind (had blank leaves mistakenly bound in). Cohen remarked that, had he actually been there to witness this discovery, he would not have been able to continue writing poems. His mock-tragic persona was beginning to acquire followers in the U.S. as well, though he was still known primarily as a poet, a title that lent plausibility to his image and justified it. He had not yet become a full-time legend.

One of the marks of Cohen's career has been his willingness to extend himself into other forms. This characteristic eventually helped him make the transition to songwriting more naturally. But it also enabled him to contribute to radio and television shows and write two film scores (for *Angel*, a National Film Board short, in 1966, and for Robert Altman's *McCabe and Mrs. Miller*, in 1971).

His first excursion outside poetry came in 1963 with his novel *The Favourite Game*, which was first published in Britain and was, as George Woodcock has pointed out, a poet's novel, full of idle phrasemaking and upper-case Writing. At one point in the narrative, for instance, Braverman, the lecherous protagonist, watches helplessly as one of his meticulously planned seductions goes awry at the crucial moment. He feels "like an archaeologist watching the sand blow back." Braverman is portrayed as a thoroughly middle-class, suburban character; the novel is thus Cohen momentarily letting down his guard, exposing the classless, saintly pose for what it was but using another component of his persona — penitence — for heightened and comic effect. Braverman is a loser but not a beautiful loser. The material world is too much with him, at the expense of the spiritual. The book is a literary novel trying to be popular, a fact that speaks a great deal of Cohen's complicated identity at the time. He tottered towards respectability as a writer while struggling with the desire to be a legend instead.

A year after *The Favourite Game* he published a third collection of poetry, *Flowers for Hitler*, in which his verse forms were freer than before and his rhythms fit perfectly the mercurial romantic despair characteristic of his most memorable poems (and later some of his least distinctive songs). The new metric freedom, however, seems in retrospect as much a device for inflating his image as for changing the direction of his writing. Reading the book now, one can see him edging towards songwriting; one can delight in the lyrics but even more in the tussle with lyricism. Here Cohen's persona has bloomed. He poses as an antediluvian character full of tired wisdom only occasionally relieved by some bright perception of sex.

At that point he also displays fully for the first time the down-at-heel religiosity that would later be predominant. Cohen sometimes appears to abolish the hyphen in the phrase Judeo-Christian tradition. Christ and God serve the function in his writing of spirits whose purity Cohen, a mere kinky mortal, can never match, however much he continues trying. These spirits serve him as the machinery served Chaplin in *Modern Times*: they allow for pratfalls. The process lets Cohen admit to self-indulgent and sentimental lapses which are then incorporated into the list of ailments destroying him and making him a martyr. Spirituality is a device for pathos and romanticism, so that, for him, Jesus and Shelley carry much the same distinction as beautiful losers.

Flowers for Hitler, which won the most important Quebec literary prize of the day, sent Cohen off again on the poetry circuit. He had been giving public readings since the 1950s, and travelling on such tours helped to make him known while laying the groundwork for the transitional period in which he sang before audiences as well as read to them. The 1964 tour, however, would have considerable effect on the speed with which he become a legend and professional personality foremost. The publisher Jack McClelland had reprinted *Let Us Compare Mythologies* as part of what became, in effect, a uniform edition of his poetical works, and then with characteristic enterprise planted with the National Film Board the idea of filming a tour by Cohen and other poets on his list, including Layton and Earle Birney. Donald Brittain and Don Owen shot a great deal of footage before deciding that much of it involving the other poets was too uneven or otherwise unsuitable. To salvage the project they turned what remained into *Ladies and Gentlemen . . . Mr. Leonard Cohen*, which became the first important vehicle for Cohen's multidisciplinary image.

Perhaps 1966 was the last year in which Cohen was primarily a literary figure, albeit one who was more famous than read, despite publishing two books that year. The first was a new poetry collection, *Parasites of Heaven*, which if only by its title shows that he was expanding and refining the artfully got-up tragic pose he had developed for himself. The other was his novel *Beautiful Losers* which was received in Canada with nearly unanimous hostility and only slowly came to occupy an important position as a postmodernist classic: a book written in such a full-out way, with all his anguished spirituality and sense of alienation, that his early work would forever seem just a blueprint for it, and all that came later (mostly music) a pale copy of the original. It was almost as though the book were his rude farewell gesture at the literary world that had brought him out of the shadows but could never satisfy (or take seriously?) his craving for artistic flagellation. A year later, he recorded his first album.

The critics and literary people who, however guardedly they praised his work, had taken him in as an initiate in their order, generally were hostile to the success he found as a singer and songwriter. His old McGill mentor Louis Dudek lamented the way in which "genuine artists of promise descend perforce to mere entertainment and become idols or celebrities like Leonard Cohen, who was a fine poet before he 'gave all that up' to take up the guitar." Others, less bluntly, mourned the loss or at least were intrigued by the transition. But Cohen was concerned with the aesthetics of pretending to be washed-up, a theme he had claimed in *Beautiful Losers* and has not really let go of since. It was almost as though cultivating obsolescence was his way of dealing with the Canadian response to his success. Lightfoot might be famous for being, despite his popularity, shy. So Cohen achieved fame for always seeming to be fraught to the point of nervous collapse with nightmares of inadequacy. And at least one small part of his mythology of human frailty and incompetence is the exaggerated story of how unprepared he was for a career in music.

Cohen was signed by Columbia Records in 1967, once Judy Collins had recorded "*Suzanne*" to considerable success; she was becoming known as a star-maker as her version of "*Both Sides Now*" brought fame to Joni Mitchell. For its part, Columbia was coming to the forefront of popular music, as its new president, Clive Davis, moved the company away from classical releases, Broadway cast albums, and Mitch Miller singalongs. He was creating, partly through his association with *Rolling Stone*, the notion that Columbia, while certainly part of a big conglomerate, was nonetheless the home of hip alternate-culture capitalism: a genuine cultural advantage at the time. John Hammond, the famous A&R who signed Cohen, was ridiculed for encouraging such an apparently unmu ulcul property — but ridiculed gently because, after all, he had signed Dylan six years earlier. Hammond, though, knew full well the problems involved in Cohen's lack of musicianship, perhaps even foreseeing the way studio musicians would laugh throughout the first recording session. But he was correct in thinking that Cohen could be made into a highly profitable legend. It was common at this time for people to look up to certain singer-songwriters — Dylan of course but also Paul Simon and many others — as poets, a reckless accolade calculated to bring echoes from linear poets who felt threatened. Here, in Cohen, was an opportunity to make a songpoet of someone already respected as a real poet. In the context of 1967 that must have seemed a brilliant idea.

Like all such breaks, however, Cohen's Columbia signing was, from his point of view, only the payoff to a long process of hard work, not the capricious result of some record company executive and some hustler of an agent going to lunch together, for his musical roots extended much further back than was commonly known. He began playing guitar as an adolescent at a socialist summer camp north of Montreal and knew more of the instrument than he let on, judging from the testimony of some to whom he gave lessons, such as Max Layton, Irving's son. If he was no Springsteen, edging into songwriting from a career as a versatile session hand and all-purpose musician, neither was he a Carl Sandburg, sidelining in music for years with an absolute minimum of chords and practically no right-hand technique. By the early 1950s Cohen was in a trio called the Buckskin Boys and by the middle of the decade was part of bohemia where folk music was important to the type of sensibility its residents were cultivating. People from the period recall him at parties singing Spanish Civil War songs as well as Jewish folksongs of the sort then being made popular by Theodore Bikel, who frequently played at the Ritz Carlton.

One witness says that although the theory was never articulated, everyone in Cohen's circle tended to believe in Dm, Em, and Am as the three basic chords rather than C, D, and G major. The whole atmosphere they created for themselves seemed best couched in the minor mode, a sensibility from which Cohen has never strayed far, though the continued allegiance may have something to do with his knack for building strength from weakness even while celebrating it, and for disguising musical faults as so many emotional excellences. His playing is at best accompaniment, and usually only of the sort that serves as background. Similarly, his voice has a limited range, most often being stuck at the lowest end of the scale. But such shortcomings when combined with his prosody, and the way the two boost each other, make his music distinctive. Cohen's songs have a strong oriental streak, in the older sense of the word oriental. He has been accused of writing tunes with all the melodic volatility of Gregorian chants, and indeed many of the songs are chant-like, but this works to their advantage. When changes come, they are timed to coincide with a line of the lyric he wishes to emphasize. He achieved a sort of tuneful dissonance early on, though few of his melodies would survive the test of being worthwhile instrumentals. As *Rolling Stone* once commented, Cohen always seems to be setting melodies to completed lyrics, not the reverse.

It is easy to imagine the dilemma that faced John Simon, the producer assigned to work with the artist on what became that first album, SONGS OF LEONARD COHEN. Here was a fine lyricist all right, but he had a voice that faded like the white dot that lingers in the centre of an old TV screen once the power has been switched off, and he played, but only competently, a classical guitar, an instrument he had never grown away from because the nylon strings were easier on his fingers and better suited to his gentler songs. The album clearly would have to be based not on performing talent but on a need to communicate that transcended mere ability. Listening to Cohen would have to be like eavesdropping on some famous and tragic figure from the past. The production somehow would have to keep tedium out of rapt attention's way. About the only production touch was a female chorus interceding eerily, and comically, in an attempt to support Cohen's failing voice. Cohen first said he found its presence disquieting but later incorporated a similar chorus into his concerts. It wasn't long before the posters for his spring European tours promised the opportunity of seeing "the legendary Leonard Cohen."

Other writers of the time, Joni Mitchell for one, also rose to prominence after having their songs recorded by second parties (in her case, by Tom Rush and later Dylan as well as Judy Collins). Once established, they struck out on their own, writing more complex, less generalized and far more intensely personal material bearing their own stamp and no one else's. They put so much of themselves into the writing and recording of what were, in effect, the authorized versions that few other artists could cover them. In some ways, there is a distinction to be made here between the artist in song and the tunesmith who may or may not be an artist as well. For instance, alongside Cohen, Gordon Lightfoot is mainly a tunesmith, while the Beatles are tunesmiths as well as artists of personal and group statement of a particularly high order; Cohen is unusual in being an artist first and very little second, making it difficult for other, more accomplished performers to record his later work, at least until Jennifer Warnes rose to the task so memorably. Of that generation, Judy Collins was practically

"A single individual facing the tide of events, Cohen must content himself with love — or at least sex — among the ruins."

the last important progressive musician whose primary role was interpretative rather than creative. Even she failed to find much recordable material in Cohen after his second and third albums, SONGS FROM A ROOM and SONGS OF LOVE AND HATE. In the two decades he has been recording, Cohen may seem to have undergone musical changes without having progressed very far, but in fact he has slowly refined his image to the point where his literary self and his musical self are one. He has become an original by becoming less an originator than a perpetuator and caretaker of what he has already created. So much of the impact of his music depends on the air of mystery and sense of wanton fragility he has built around himself.

In a nice little bit of synchronicity, that first album, SONGS OF LEONARD COHEN, appeared in January 1968, within a month of Dylan's JOHN WESLEY HARDING. The two somehow go together in memory, perhaps in part because they share a tone, one less spiritual than biblical and less inspirational than ecclesiastic (which Cohen continues to work with long after Dylan moved on, came back, then moved on again, as is his custom). Dylan achieved the sound through clever though simple arrangements and melodic diversity, adding a sense of urgency into the bargain. Cohen arrived at it as a result of his habitual plodding along from one cut to the next, using his monotone to restate what fancy production values and greater dexterity would have lessened. Central to the album is the fact that it not only strives to recapture live sound but to duplicate a live session, with all the errors and poor takes. The mixture heightens the illusion of spontaneity. On *"Suzanne,"* for instance, Cohen's breath control is, at times, out of sync with the flow of the melody, as might be expected when a middle-length poem is being translated into another medium. On the recorded version the lines "And she feeds you tea and oranges / That come all the way from China" come out "And she [short breath] feeds you tea and oranges / That come [short breath] all [short breath] the way from China." Yet at other times the control is perfect, as when he rises unexpectedly on a particularly striking image or lets himself trail off like the sound of bus air-brakes to indicate what, on the printed page, would be "et cetera."

His diction is generally clear, but there is a constant ambivalence in his pronunciation that can be attributed to his Canadian upbringing as well as to his casual approach to recording. *"The Stranger Song"* contains the lines, "And then taking from his wallet / An old schedule of trains, he'll say / 'I told you when I came I was a stranger.' " Cohen pronounces the ninth word the American way, as *skedul*, rather than as *shedule*, as you would expect an English Montrealer from McGill of the 1950s to do. But he does so, significantly, only after a minisecond's hesitation, as though genuinely uncertain. Similarly, in "*Sisters of Mercy*" he sings "Oh I hope you run into them / You who've *bin* travelling so long," but later in the same cut comes, "Well, I've *bean* where you're hanging / I think I can see how you're pinned."

Many of his poems were short lyrics without refrains which are not easily put to music. The exceptions in terms of length and construction were "*Suzanne*" and "*Master Song.*" The latter had to be rewritten a bit to flow better musically and to acknowledge changing times. (The line "You meet him at some temple where they take your clothes at the door" had first read "at some nightclub.") He had to learn to write longer single verses which kept to the point and were free-standing statements, not pastiches of clever lines and images, the only alternative being to write short verses linked by choruses. He succeeded at both but only at the price of emphasizing his old tendency to use imagery to lead the reader through a maze of commonplaces. In his early songwriting, this weakness became the habit of overextending a metaphor or weaving in and out between a couple of them, then trying to compensate by using too much repetition in the melody line. There are examples in "*The Stranger Song*" and "*Sisters of Mercy.*" Later, beginning with the third album, SONGS OF LOVE AND HATE, he tried to overcome the limitation by writing longer songs (though one that was short as well as upbeat, "*Diamonds in the Mine,*" was the only distinctive melody as such). These slower and more lugubrious songs with their complicated patterns of imagery were less romantic by nature, in fact more doggedly anti-romantic. In such ones as "*Dress Rehearsal Rag,*" "*Last Year's Man,*" "*Famous Blue Raincoat,*" and "*Avalanche,*" he was not trying to put a definite shape to the public identity he had created, becoming the only figure in pop music to traffic in the appearance of being an intellectual by design rather than some accident of nature. Whereas Paul Simon sang of reading Robert Frost and Bob Dylan referred to Rimbaud and Verlaine, Cohen quoted only himself. He seemed to have a fully matured world view, for his art is nearly always more compelling than his artifice.

Randy Newman also wrote a song called "*Suzanne.*" Before singing it in concert he would often remind the audience that "it's not to be confused with Leonard Cohen's song of the same title — Leonard's is conducted on a far higher moral plane." Cohen's musical personality consists of assuming the romantic viewpoint of Jacques Brel and the *chansonniers* then coating it with poetic religiosity and sorrow at the human condition. In some ways the result does indeed amount to a moral stance. Usually, though, it is something more nebulous and more complicated — his anti-image — which sometimes appears contrived but at other times seems the outpouring of a temperament he has cultivated in profoundly legitimate ways.

That the somewhat artificial public Cohen occasionally hides behind wit and satire does not always make it easy to separate him from the artist who uses the same qualities as raw material. The two Cohens are almost as difficult to pull apart as some of the various GBS's that George Bernard Shaw used in similar ways. Because Cohen is indeed an artist, writing however coyly, means that clues can be found more easily in his work itself than in his comments on it.

Unlike Gordon Lightfoot, Joni Mitchell, or even Neil Young, Cohen is not a product of the folk-music revival of the early and middle 1960s. His roots are in 1950s culture generally, in which a smaller and more sober folk-music underground had a place. In this allegiance he resembles his teacher Irving Layton who is forever stamped with the seal of Canada in the 1950s when the shout of rebellion was less distinct than it was in the U.S. but, because mass complacency was perhaps less topical, and more a permanent fact of life, the need for protest was all the greater. Cohen thus resembles the early Beat poets, before they came to be styled as such; he is lost somewhere in the tragi-romantic spell of Dylan Thomas and others who, however tame they seem now, were considered daring infidels by the Beats whom Cohen came of age admiring from afar. Also, Cohen's music owed little to other professional performers, unlike that of the folksong revivalists who followed; it came from amateur performers who perhaps got some of it from actual folk or at least wished they had.

Aesthetic considerations aside, then, his music is not supposed to be professional or innovative; it's meant to perpetuate past attitudes and feelings. Therefore the quality of his singing is determinedly non-professional, since, if polished, his music would lose its historical and personal context. Significantly, when he sang on the soundtrack of *McCabe and Mrs. Miller*, he actually sounded like an old-fashioned traditional folksinger, with a craggy, rich brown voice, though he wasn't doing anything differently than he does in concert, where his appearance and stage manner detract from the impression. Equally revealing is the fact that when a music publisher issued a collection of Cohen's songs arranged especially for folk-style guitar, the arrangements were almost identical to those in the earlier songbooks in which folk styles had not been used.

So although Cohen as a poet bore some resemblance to the American Beats, he was far too romantic about the wrong things, too conventional, and despaired less of the times than of himself; he was closer to the British poets. The resemblance between him and the early Allen Ginsberg, for instance, is purely one of shared belief in the 1950s bohemian style in general, whereas the differences are important ones of intent and priority. Cohen, for instance, does not have Ginsberg's scholarly nature, though his longing to identify with a kind of scholarship based on arcane lore is one of the elements of *Beautiful Losers*. Again unlike Ginsberg, he is no pantheist but only seems to be. On his LIVE SONGS album there is a country tune, "*Passing Through*," which at first seems like a pretty convincing redneck hymn but on examination sounds that way not because of the music but because of the pop-on-the-way-to-populist lyrics, its theology so unsophisticated as to be naïve, in keeping with one's notions of what holyrollers would play on their truck tapedecks en route to the Dixie Drive-In.

Left to write in his own mode, Cohen is painfully conscious of the slipping away of tradition and the loss of his own youth. He seems fearful of disappointing ancestors he has never met and of sliding into irrelevance himself. A song such as "*Chelsea Hotel No. 2*," in the way the lyric juxtaposes the warm past with the hollowness that has replaced it, is almost a kind of nostalgia for the present, the ultimate absurdity in the instant culture he rejects and regrets. To change the subject is only to come at the argument from a different angle, so that songs like "*The Old Revolution*" emphasize how emotional (not eschatological) his writings are, how decadent (not realistic or naturalist) his manner, how his politics, whatever they might be, advocate most forcefully the return to a personal past. Two strains in his work, two pieces of shorthand, are endurance and vulnerability. His individualism is of a particularly cosmopolitan kind, but he sets himself up as an Horatio Alger hero gone full cycle, a rags-to-riches-to-rags-again story, a self-destroyed rather than a self-made man. He is insistent about the struggle to assert himself as an individual in a society from which he is operating at cross-purposes, searching for beauty where only ugliness abounds. His songs are like plants, nourished by the surrounding decomposition. In this, they mesh perfectly with his anti-image.

It was fifteen years ago that everything started to come apart for Leonard Cohen, and so to come together, too.

Consider the situation. In 1973, when his recording life was already beginning to sag in the North American market, and when much of his audience associated "Leonard Cohen books" with the various songsheets, he published a new literary work, *The Energy of Slaves*, a collection of poems that not only re-emphasized but practically crystallized what would come to seem the shortcomings of his later verse. It was almost a reminder of the suggestion that, by writing *Beautiful Losers*, a masterpiece about the impossibility of producing masterpieces, he had washed his hands of the literary world that had always sought to explain or adopt him and thus reduce the potency of his image. The poems were no better crafted than those that songwriters once delighted in printing on record jackets as so many imaginative leftovers, but there was a photograph that said much of Cohen's position. It showed him with his head shaved, like a convict or a penitent, standing in simple clothes, like a holy man or a beggar, in a room that could be a morgue, a public toilet, or a crematorium. Such is the way he chose to appear in the period when his power was in disrepute, when the critic and poet Dennis Lee, while implying praise for a few of Cohen's individual poems, suggested that his romanticism and lack of depth would ultimately put him in much the same league as Bliss Carman. But all Carman ever tried to be was a happy romantic poet. Cohen's success lay in appearing to be less prosperous and more melancholy as time went on. He was true to some 1950s archetype, Charlie Parker perhaps, one of those tragic figures whose most remarkable feature is the ability to wrest such fine work from so hellish a private life (though whether Cohen suffers all the anguish his songs indicate is an unanswerable question).

Such was the picture Cohen presented at the time of *Energy of Slaves* and such albums as LIVE SONGS and NEW SKIN FOR THE OLD CEREMONY: a kind of anti-celebrity, a walking ghost tugging at people's sleeves to tell them of his earthly life. He apparently had tired of being an elite artist, whose message and craft go together to make a precious object that transcends its creator's personality, and became instead the literary and musical equivalent of a conceptual artist, in whom the personality and the work are one — and more important than the object itself, which is impermanent, biodegradable almost. His pet concerns, such as individual dereliction or the failure of love, grew until they could no longer be called subject matter. By writing and performing songs, or simply standing on stage forlornly, he communicated this personality to the audience, which was too caught up in the mood and perhaps too musically unsophisticated to pay much attention to the structure of the songs. He was thus using the commonest technology available to him (the guitar) to bypass the critical process and by that very method to interact with the public directly. That could almost be a definition of conceptualism.

Having come to conceptualism, he couldn't bow to formal organization any longer. Working in that manner, he couldn't write technically success-ful songs or poems about failure. The songs or poems actually had to *be* failures. So it was that, beginning in the early 1970s, he produced albums and books which were, technically and poetically, failures of a high order and hence, in this scheme of things, successes in their own terms. It was as though he were saying, "The mere fact that I can work under such depressing conditions tells the story. The result is merely proof for those who need it." There was still an intimate and intricate connection between his musical self and his literary self, but it was more complicated now than it had ever been. In 1977 he was planning to bring out a book called *Death of a Ladies' Man* but at the last minute postponed publication for a year, until after the album of the same name had appeared. If both works fail in their apparent aim of being unsuccessful (which for the most part they do not), it is because there were still occasional, almost atavistic flashes of the old Cohen. The title, for instance, is practically the quintessential

"As he has grown older, Cohen has used the concept of advancing years to reinforce the image of the tortured and disconsolate soul."

one for something by Cohen, though it also seems to refer to what, at one point in the text, is his rather late-coming realization that "it's stupid to be a man," not a woman. Also it could almost be taken as a prescient segue into the AIDS references in "*Everybody Knows*" on the I'M YOUR MAN album. Then too there were certain choice lines (about how he "wept in a general way for the fate of men") which remind us of a younger Cohen, who was forever weeping in a general way and confessing to nothing in particular. At base, though, these were pieces by a writer who, having once abandoned literature for music, now seemed to be forsaking music for a cult of despair which the songs helped to deliver but not to shape.

This, an MBA might say, is his position in the market: he's skilled at giving the impression of deterioration, an appearance that's integral to his public acceptance; and just as popular music requires him to be, if not a poet, then at least one who gives the suggestion of poetry, so it necessitates his always seeming to be on the very brink of disintegration.

An odd figure, Cohen, and one who lets little information about his personal life reach the public. Most of his early followers, for example, are unaware that he and the Marianne to whom several memorable songs are addressed were actually married. How torturously he writes about personal and private relationships without quite distinguishing one from another. He names names — Suzanne, Marianne, Nancy — but they are practically interchangeable to everyone but himself; he is confessional in only the most non-specific way. Similarly, one often hears reports about his movements, that he has been in Los Angeles or entered a Zen monastery, or just earned a black belt, or is considering giving up something important, but one seldom comes into possession of any new facts. Each interview he does, when he grants one at all, has fewer details than the last. He chooses to communicate by gossip and allegation, and though it is only a lifelong rumour, one suspects it is true that this style too is a part of the manipulation of his own image. In fairness, though, the image needs a lot of substance behind it. Without that, no one would have been interested in his shadow for so long.

No doubt the cultural and emotional concerns of his songs are quite real to him. They do not always end up as the subjects of his music, however; sometimes they are used for self-ridicule. He jokes about himself much the way a fat person tells fat jokes to forestall similar jibes from others. Age is one topic for such humour. He is one of those basically decadent writers who has long affected greater worldweariness than strict chronology would entitle him to. When he started to record he was already thirty-three, far older than his audience, to say nothing of his colleagues (even Dylan was younger by the better part of a generation). The age factor directed him to certain approaches in music. Amateur musicians or late arrivals on the scene (Linda McCartney is a good example) tended to be hooted down, and Cohen was forced to assume a musical fundamentalism from the start. As late as 1975, in the notes to his BEST OF LEONARD COHEN album, he acknowledged graciously that "Ron Cornelius helped me with a chord change in an early version" of "*Chelsea Hotel*," an admission that would have been humiliating to anyone else successful enough to have a greatest-hits album.

As he has grown older, Cohen has used the concept of advancing years to reinforce the image of the tortured and disconsolate soul. By the middle and later 1970s he was setting himself up as a visitor from long ago. And as he has aged, he has come abreast of his early reputation. He may incur disfavour with his methodology or his outlook (Jennifer Warnes's manager warned her not to sing such gloomy stuff). But the more remote he becomes from the rest of the scene, the more vital his image among people more interested in him than modern music in general, the people who have always accounted for the better part of his large following. They seem to take the gradual decline as an indication of the development of his personality and his philosophy. They are probably correct.

Cohen's falling out of favour as a literary person caused him to dedicate most of his talent to songs. Throughout the 1970s the increasingly sophisticated field of pop criticism made him appear a more spiritual musician, less concerned with professionalism than with carrying on a search for salvation. For the price of a record or tape you can overhear the mumblings of a seeker. It might seem at times as though the better part of his art is beating dead horses. In fact, he is a kind of mirror-image Godot, always present, forever about to disappear on some journey of discovery. It is a curiously contemporary irony, and maybe a particularly Canadian one, that if he could ever achieve the goal it would surely be his ruination.

If you were to happen upon a large portion of his work in isolation, without any prior knowledge of Cohen as a writer and performer, you might put him squarely within the recognizable seventeenth-century tradition of incoherent babbling about the Old Testament. Unlike his mentor Irving Layton, who so often excoriated Christians for anti-Semitism, Cohen has no clear viewpoint at all. His religious language has a way of both obscuring and underlining the effect of what he is trying to do, and in his most recent book, *Book of Mercy*, he uses interchangeably such terms as the Lord of Unity, Our Lady of the Torch, the Law, the king of the dead, the father of mercy, or simply the second person singular, as in, "Find me, you whom David found in hell." His political views are clearer, however: he is obviously anti-state, even when the state is "the revolt that calls itself Israel" with what he describes as its "miasmal homesteads, black Hebrew gibberish of pruned grave vines." One senses that such assertions are not meant to be controversial because they are not to be excerpted and reprinted this way; they're simply part of a larger whole in which the rhythms of devout prose are more important than the actual content. The tone often *sounds* right when the meditations are not really saying anything at all: "Though I am unwept, it is your judgement that parches me." He is not making language-centred postmodernist poetry but using language to perform a ceremony (and ceremony, like mercy, is one of his favourite words). Through such ceremony he keeps moving closer to the idea that only in personal failure can we find the humility needed to be saintly. Such is the serious subtext of his surface posturings. The result is that his work is sometimes suggestive of what Rod McKuen might have come up with if McKuen had been an artist, or what Soren Kierkegaard would have written for laughs if he had been that kind of fellow. Running against the current of the times has always suited him. He actually seems to enjoy watching his popularity recede in the periods which make the comebacks possible. Like some sort of career masochist, he has used his decline to feed still more writing about failure, trying always to sink to his lowest or rise to his highest, depending on the vantage point one takes, the audience's or Cohen's own.

I remember twenty years ago now sitting in the Toronto publishing house where I was employed when a copy of Cohen's *Selected Poems* arrived in the mail. Another of the upstart young poets who worked or loitered there began fingering it madly, flipping backwards and forwards through the section of hitherto uncollected verse at the back. Cackling with malicious glee, this writer, who often spoke in italics, kept saying, *"Look, he's written himself out! See! He's finished! I knew it! What did I tell you?"* Even on mid-length reflection it seemed a sensible judgement. A dozen years and several Cohen comebacks later, however, I ran into this same person on the street one day. He told me that he had given up writing in 1971 and was now managing a clothing store in a shopping plaza. He said he could fix me up with a nice two-piece worsted.

He gave me his card.

three

JONI MITCHELL
Back and Forth

"Mitchell is primarily a writer . . . whose influence, though indirect, has been immense."

A great deal of nonsense has been written about Joni Mitchell, some of it by Joni Mitchell herself. Her songs have formed an ongoing diary of the most personal sort. They are also practically her only public statements of any type. She has become more reclusive with the years, and interviews are now so rare that they are jumped on and dissected by followers who feel both titillated and frustrated by her insularity. This curious relationship has been going on for years. In the 1970s, the result of it was that each new record followed months of speculation, rumour, and gossip, talk which sometimes revealed as much about her life as about the albums themselves, though each release always contained a few musical surprises, just as her ones in the 1980s did. It has been that way from the start, when she made the transition from Canadian to North American, from copyright artist to star in her own right.

As an example of this peculiar process, one might look back, almost at random, at her album HEJIRA. One of the rumours predating its appearance in 1976 was that Tom Waits would sing backup on several of the numbers. With his blues cut-ups and monologues, Waits had only recently become famous for satirizing the nightlife and lowlife of Los Angeles with its cheap sex, bad food, and bloodshot eyes. The story turned out to be erroneous but is nonetheless important because having Waits on the album is exactly the sort of thing Mitchell *would* have done if she had thought of it. Waits' image was based on his being the apotheosis of sleaze. He represented, and still represents, what has become of the blues tradition in a society that many people, including a wide cross-section of Canadians, liked to believe was collapsing on itself. Mitchell seems to have spent much of her career searching for anything fashionable in the hope of discovering something she has lost. She gives the impression of being the sort of person who, were she into religion, would fondle rattlesnakes and speak in tongues — and then quit as quickly as she had begun. It is of such fleeting enthusiasms and personal disappointments (especially disappointments) that her music is made.

The speculation about her music, however, is nothing alongside that about her personal life. A feminist response to such speculation might be to criticize how she has been singled out for such public treatment in a way that her male colleagues have not been, and there is much to recommend such a reaction. Yet there is a very real sense in which Mitchell's is a special case, since much of her discontinuous musical journal is concerned with past and present lovers. Scott Fitzgerald once remarked that Hemingway seemed to require a new wife in order to write each major novel, and for a long time much the same notion was current about Mitchell; in the years between her first and second marriages, she did little if anything to discourage it. On various occasions she was "romantically linked" with Leonard Cohen, James Taylor, David Crosby, Graham Nash, Neil Young, and (inevitable on such a list) Warren Beatty. Yet for all their personal references and honesty, her songs have immense impact because of what they say of lovers generically. The majority of meaningful and important love songs (and hate songs) of recent years have been written by women. In, say, the last decade before the AIDS epidemic became a pressing concern, Mitchell, perhaps not always knowingly, stood to be one of the leading critics of contemporary sexual relations. Possibly in the late 1970s that is what being a critic of society came down to.

In all her songs, though, there is a note of detachment. There is always a reticence, a drawing back from total involvement, and a reversion to mere poetics, to verse without substance. Such hesitation is what gives her lyrics their special objectivity and appeal, and it is tempting to speculate that the pulling back is somehow tied to her being Canadian. She is part of a certain stratum of American society, yet removed from it; she is an outsider who wants to be on the inside but has sense enough not to be. This ambivalence comes through in many of her songs and places her in literary as well as musical tradition — as part of the long list of British and European travellers who, beginning after the American Revolution, published journals of their sojourns in the New World, whose stumbling towards democracy they viewed with apprehension, bewilderment, cultural confusion, and sometimes grudging admiration. Full of awe at the potential of the United States and despair at the actualities she has slowly come to see as her own, Mitchell is, in that sense, a kind of rock 'n' roll Tocqueville.

She was born Roberta Joan Anderson in 1943 in Fort Macleod, Alberta, where her father was serving with the Royal Canadian Air Force. He was later stationed in Calgary and in Yorkton, Saskatchewan. After his discharge he moved his family first to North Battleford, Saskatchewan, and finally to Saskatoon. Like Judy Collins, Mitchell was stricken with polio as a child, though she recovered after about one year, when she was ten. Otherwise, from all accounts, hers was the typical Prairie girlhood of the kind enshrined in Canadian fiction. She showed an early talent in the graphic arts, which her parents duly encouraged her to develop. Following high school in Saskatoon she enrolled in the Alberta College of Art in Calgary but, in the end, remained there only a year. She found the curriculum too constricting and was eager to put her energies into music, which was slowly coming to occupy her time.

That was in 1962, and a word should be said about the musical climate in which she then found herself. It was for the most part a mediocre period, popular music being almost entirely defined by what was heard on AM radio. Much of what now is remembered from the early 1960s is cherished either as pure nostalgia or as so much rock history. The radio audience had not yet achieved much sophistication and fell for all sorts of singers whose careers were little more than the result of some clever promoter, in the professional jargon of the period, doing a Fabian; the youthful allegiance that made possible a Bobby Rydell seems preposterously misplaced.

There was another element at work as well. Slowly at first, but with remarkable swiftness, folk was edging its way into the mainstream. In radio terms, this probably began in 1956 with the Kingston Trio's "*Tom Dooley*," a much prettified version of the old folk song "*Tom Doula*," and within a few years folk became a major force. Although by 1962 the revival had brought folk purists out of the bushes, the scene was still dominated by the Kingston Trio and other bland commercialized groups such as the Chad Mitchell Trio and Peter, Paul and Mary, the best of the lot, whom Albert Grossman had brought together in a calculated updating of the Fabian star-making technique. In 1962 the Beatles were still largely unknown outside Liverpool and Hamburg, and Bob Dylan had just released his first album. Until 1964–65, when the Beatles hit North America and Dylan moved away from acoustic work, folk existed as a sort of delightful purgatory into which one ascended from the underworld of AM teeny rock.

As far as recorded music went, folk appeared on albums to the near exclusion of 45s, thus helping to pave the way for FM radio. Characteristically, though, folk was not a radio phenomenon at all but flourished in the coffee houses and small clubs that sprang up in the larger cities and in practically every university town. Because of her age and because she was moving in "serious" art-school circles, Mitchell was drawn into folk without having grown up in the world of AM radio, as did people only a few years older (Dylan, for instance) who had lived in the United States or the more populous centres of Canada.

As a girl Mitchell had studied piano but had had no experience with guitar. Until she mastered it, she sang folk songs accompanying herself on the ukulele (Eric Clapton and David Byrne began the same way). She frequented coffee houses such as the Louis Riel in Saskatoon and The Depression in Calgary, and soon began performing in them as well. She presented herself at this time in what now seems an incongruous image — a pigtailed soprano, doing old English and American folk songs in the manner of already established figures such as Joan Baez and Judy Collins, whose madonna-like images her own experience in no way justified. Without being urban, she was imitating the urban folk singers who were themselves imitating rural artists of long ago. Without being an intellectual, she was copying the intellectuals who sought in the popular music of other eras to dissociate themselves from the masses of the present. She became part of what Wilfrid Mellens, one of her most perceptive critics, would call, in his book *Angels of the Night: Popular Female Singers of Our Time* (1976), "the New Eve's search for social and creative identity in her New Ethnic Garden."

At first, she was good at what she did without being a professional. The move towards professionalism, and away from folk towards songs of her own, came in 1965 after a visit to Toronto. Early that year she decided to journey east to the annual Mariposa Folk Festival, which was then being held at Innis Lake, north of Toronto (before it found the permanent site on the Toronto Islands by which it is remembered). On the long train trip across the Prairies and through the Lakehead she wrote her first song, "*Day by Day.*" It was, like so many people's first song, a blues piece, inspired, she said later, by the rhythm of the train wheels. One evening after a session at the festival she stumbled into a rooming house run by the printmaker and future video artist Vera Frenkel. The house, something of a gathering place for local artists, was on Huron Street in the Annex area of the city, and on this occasion a party was in progress. One of the occupants, a Nigerian prince who had come to Canada to do graduate studies, was overly sensitive to noise and went downstairs to discover Mitchell playing guitar in the bathroom. She was prevailed upon to join the celebration. Participants remember that at this, probably her first Toronto performance, she sang many songs alone and with others, including the unbearably overworked "*Jacob's Ladder*" — which gives some hint of her repertoire at the time.

As it happened, she and the other occupants of the house got on well, and Mitchell decided to remain in Toronto. She lived on Huron Street and used it as a base for developing the beginnings of a career. She had arrived a relatively unsophisticated small-towner, replete with a scrapbook of family photographs and clippings about her high school graduation and prom, but she quickly displayed a persistence and seriousness that disowned such naïveté. She began working the non-union clubs, though not with her own material, even though by this time she had begun writing eagerly. Her left-hand technique was still uncertain; her long fingers seemed to straddle the frets like spiders, as though cast in one position by years of staccato piano exercises. She was trying also to improve her vocal range. The transition from the high reaches to the low was very awkward, and she was writing at least partly to provide herself with a body of material to suit her own voice. Frenkel remembers her saying, "I don't want to be the poor man's Joan Baez."

To work the better clubs she needed a union card. In order to pay her dues she took a job selling women's coats at Simpsons downtown, where she wore her hair in a bun with a net. At length an old Saskatoon boyfriend followed her to Toronto, and she moved out of her room to share space in the same house with another woman who later went to New York and joined Andy Warhol's menagerie. At one point, Frenkel remembers, there were three pregnant women in the house at the same time.

Perhaps the best of the coffee houses lining Yorkville Avenue and Avenue Road in those days was the Riverboat, run by Bernie Fiedler, who later became owner of a record label and the management company that handled such artists as Murray McLauchlan and Dan Hill. Like nearly everyone else in the rooming house, Mitchell for a time washed dishes at the Riverboat. Eventually she was allowed to perform there, as well as at other establishments in Yorkville Village. At one of these, the Penny Farthing, she met Chuck Mitchell, an American folksinger. They were married in June 1965 and by the end of the year had moved to Detroit. Although the marriage lasted only a short while, she was now firmly planted in the U.S. which, for all the local renown she received towards the end of her Toronto stay, was to be the base of her reputation.

Through 1966 she played the Detroit-area coffee houses and also began writing the first of what later would prove to be successful songs, such as "*The Circle Game*," whose title presumably came from Margaret Atwood's poetry collection of the same name which received the Governor General's Award for that year. She received excellent notices, and with them came offers to play the poorly paid but prestigious circuit, especially New York. Al Kooper, the scamp musician associated with Blood, Sweat and Tears and the Blues Project, has painted a memorable picture of Mitchell at this time, as a timid but dedicated unknown whose talent was even more striking than her vulnerability. In 1967 she was playing for $115 a week at the Café au Go Go where she was spotted by the manager Elliot Roberts. He negotiated her first recording contract, with the Reprise label, on which she would record four albums before switching to Asylum in 1972. It was shortly after completing the first of these, JONI MITCHELL, that she moved from New York to Los Angeles, a place with which she would become closely identified, despite her many musical dissimilarities from what is ordinarily thought of as the Los Angeles sound. Indeed, her connection with the sound appears to have come initially through personal relationships. Her first LP was produced by David Crosby (with Stephen Stills one of the session men). Crosby was then still identified with the Byrds, a band that, with its rock versions of Dylan songs, was making unfashionable the kind of polite folk-like classicism Mitchell practiced and that, together with the Beach Boys, the Mamas and the Papas, and a few other groups, was at the centre of a new West Coast movement. Mitchell's music always seems to undergo various changes and improvements only after gaining fresh power from other musicians.

That first album, which was made up entirely of her own songs, was still very much in the acoustic folk idiom, and appeared in 1968 at the tail end of the unchallenged heyday of such music. It was divided into two parts: the first side, headed "I came to the city," was given over to New York-inspired songs; the other, entitled "Out of the city and down to the seaside," was culled from experience on the Coast. It was a successful integration of the two and also a critical and financial success for a first LP. Yet it is a curious fact that Mitchell's reputation at the time was owed to other people's versions of her songs, which she herself would not record until much later. Such copyright songs were far less personal than those on the album; they smacked of highblown prosody and were commercially suited to other performers. Tom Rush, for example, recorded "*Tin Angel*," "*The Circle Game*," and "*Urge for Going*," and Buffy Sainte-Marie released versions of "*The Circle Game*" and "*Ode to a Seagull*." The latter was actually on the Mitchell album, as was "*Michael from Mountains*" which was recorded by Judy Collins, whose version of another Mitchell song, "*Both Sides Now*," became a hit and was the most important single development in Mitchell's career. Her songs were eventually recorded by many others as well, including Gordon Lightfoot, Dave Van Ronk, Johnny Cash, and (the ultimate accolade) Bob Dylan. It helps to locate the peak of her influence to point out that by 1973 her copyrights were estimated to be worth one and a half million dollars but by 1975 twice that amount. Such successes, however, came long after she had ceased being mainly or even incidentally a writer of songs for other people and instead began specializing in the diary-like songs whose personal intensity, difficult rhythms, and complicated vocal phrasing meant that she alone could record them.

Not until 1969 did she record some of the songs other people had made famous for her. This came about on her second album, CLOUDS. In retrospect, it seems an immensely clever way for a young singer-song-writer to have operated, since by that time she had Collins' single to help sales, to say nothing of the publicity generated by the other covers. Even so, she was still almost as much a folk performer as a rockish one and, partly as a result, not yet in the first rank of popularity, though she was getting there quickly. That same year she was the opening act for a national tour by Crosby, Stills and Nash (Neil Young had not yet become a partner on the firm's letterhead). Once the tour ended, she and Graham Nash set up housekeeping together in a modest mansion in Laurel Canyon.

From this period one can date the emergence of the diarist and the decline of the free-market tunesmith. From this point on one sees Mitchell beginning to live her life in public; for despite her increasing reclusiveness, it was through growth of the rock gossip mill that the audience began to

"Mitchell is . . . a kind of rock 'n' roll Tocqueville."

strongly identify with her as an individual and to search out the auto-
biography in the music.

What followed was a near soap opera, with Joni, the wounded Scorpio,
popping up constantly in the papers and magazines and, in another guise
and dimension, appearing each year with an album full of songs apparently wrung painfully from the very experience — sexual, emotional, or
geographical — about which its eager buyers had been reading and
gossiping. Two themes would emerge in her music. The first is representative and well thumbed, and concerns her lovers. Disciples would recite
evidence that such and such a line refers to this or that man, later discarded
or gone away. Such activity reached something like a peak following her
break-up with Nash. Then there was her struggle to adjust to California
life, which convinced the rest of the nation (and Canada) of her sensitivity
and her usefulness as a symbol for the changing role of women. She came
closest to cataloguing her dilemmas, if not to resolving them, with her
1970 album LADIES OF THE CANYON, which features songs about various
Southern California female friends and acquaintances who represent both
the seven faces of Mitchell, and the various LA types whom only the
perpetual outsider, reporter-like, could home-in on and describe. The
album went gold.

She seemed to be compounding professional success upon success
from personal confusion and uncertainty. Then, later in the year, she
announced her retirement from concerts and perhaps from careers generally. There were stories, later verified in a couple of rare interviews,
about living on Crete with a multicultural hodgepodge of alternative
culture purists; then stories of her retiring to British Columbia where she
did indeed build, with the local artisans, a stone house on forty acres of
land, to which she would often retreat in order to write. Most of her time,
however, was spent travelling in Europe. In the end she made a public
appearance at Mariposa for old time's sake. The publicity strike was
broken. Not unexpectedly, she released an album whose topics were these
travels, the recent crop of lovers, and the ongoing search for clarity and
contentment. It was entitled BLUE and would remain in some ways her
most pleasing album; at least, the one in which her melodies and lyrics,
which she had always had difficulty keeping in balance, are in agreement.
There was even one song which confesses relief (not too convincingly)
at returning to California, which she suggested, frankly but again uncon-
vincingly, she now considered home.

In 1972 she released her first Asylum album, FOR THE ROSES. It rekindled
the passions and moreover the curiosity of what had become an incredibly
loyal audience of Mitchell-watchers (who are not always the same people

whose main interest is with her music as such). Later that year she even returned to the road; her opening act (for now she was indisputably the star attraction) was a then relatively unknown Jackson Browne, the younger LA singer-songwriter-narcissist who would eventually influence her music somewhat.

The chronology continues. 1973: Joni undergoes analysis and no album that year. A world grows anxious. 1974: Joni happily settles with John Guerin, the drummer of the group LA Express, in a Spanish-style Bel-Air home that has been decorated by Sally Sirkin Lewis and afterward will be featured at length in *Architecture Digest*. Then, later that year, COURT AND SPARK, a new album that wavers between displaying self-control and affording the peek-through-the-keyhole for which the audience slavers. Then, silence again, broken principally by a brief enrollment at the Naropa Institute, the Tibetan Buddhist school in Colorado. There follows MILES OF AISLES, a decidedly unsuccessful live album. Is she pulling out of Asylum? Is this a contract-breaker or is she stalling for time? Has some cataclysmic personal tragedy, so great the others pale beside it, overtaken her life and rendered her mute? Apparently not. More gossip and then, in fall 1975, a new album, THE HISSING OF THE SUMMER LAWNS, in which she tries from the standpoint of dignified maturity to relive, at times vicariously, at others not, some of her early abandon.

Still there are no interviews to speak of and hardly any public appearances; rumour, a little innuendo, and a trickle of hard fact must be substituted. In 1976 she purchases from the playwright Neil Simon, for a reported $1.6 million, a three-storey apartment building near Wilshire Boulevard, close by the Brown Derby and the Ambassador Hotel. Talk now has it that Asylum will issue a greatest hits album. If it appears it will be a curious one indeed, since her greatest hits have been other people's versions or else songs such as "*Woodstock*" and "*You Turn Me On (I'm a Radio)*" which are uncharacteristic of her later music. But a decision is made to postpone the album to allow for what she frankly admits is "part of a growing diary of work, and I guess you could say it's a progression." It appears (without Tom Waits but with Neil Young on one band), and is indeed a continuation of Joni Mitchell as a cross between the innocent and the sybarite. It is another self-portrait of Mitchell struggling to find an identity, not to say happiness, in a world that seems strange, surreal, and unresponsive to most of her listeners but is likely stranger still — at once repellent and enticing — to Mitchell herself. HEJIRA again confirms her position as the perpetual Canadian outsider in a place that keeps changing shape just when she believes she has finally brought it into focus.

After that album, though, she became, or seemed to become, a different type of artist, a different vocal personality.

Just as the great revival and commercialization of the folk song petered out, the war in Vietnam entered its hottest phase. At the time it seemed that the shift from folk to rock was the result of a mass decision to glide on the advances of Dylan as well as on those of the Beatles and all the other British rockers who followed. In retrospect, it appears as though current events, to which the folk revival had been tied, simply became too terrifying and destructive to find continued expression in the sweet-toned dulcimer and the vigorous five-string banjo.

The folk movement was the first in which women had played as important a role as men, so equal a role that not much notice was taken of the fact. Many of the leading figures were women who were accepted as major singers, per se, rather than considered condescendingly as female stars. Unlike Dylan, they did not produce a large body of important original work, but then neither did the other males. Mitchell was significant early in her career at least partly because she differed in this respect from both male and female songwriters. Judy Collins, for instance, continued to write the occasional song but remained active as an interpreter of other people's; not until 1977 did Baez release a full album of original songs, which was generally received as being too little too late. But Mitchell was different, coming as she did in 1968 when the peace movement was peaking and would soon splinter into (among others) the women's movement. Here was the first important female songwriter; at least, the first to create a prodigious body of work to equal or surpass the men then in the field without being competitive with them. What's more, Mitchell's songs were often perceived as being wondrous evocations of the feminist sensibility, though textual evidence falls short of showing her to have been even a moderate feminist. The point is not that she was overpraised or undervalued but simply that she was, from her first appearance, given an amount of serious consideration almost without precedent at the time.

So much has been written about her music and her life that one can read through all the comments as an exercise in critical botany, noting the growth rings as year by year rock is taken more seriously as a form and written about more thoughtfully. Taking the writings together as a mass, one can also perceive three trends or crosscurrents in criticism of her work. The first, articulated by Robert Christgau of *The Village Voice*, traces her development from a late-blooming folk madonna to a type of very pragmatic feminist. Next and just as common, there are the reviewers who speak of her sophistication, both melodic and lyrical, developing apace with her musical technique. Finally, in descending order of astuteness, there are the thematic reviewers content to see her as the new all-American girl, crystallizing life as they have lived it, revising her memoirs with each new album in light of more recent sensations and emotions. Nearly all this writing has been done from the American perspective which considers her Canadian background, if at all, as little more than a clever addition to the persona.

Partly what made Mitchell immediately seem unique, even before her talent justified the assumption, was the fact that she came out of a literary tradition rather than out of the musical pop culture. The result was that her lyrics seemed at once more distinctive than her melodies, as for the most part they have remained, despite the growth, general refinement and mellowing of her songwriting. By comparison, Bob Dylan and, for example, Paul Simon, despite their different poetic pretensions, were influenced mainly by radio and were already writing and playing rock 'n' roll as teenagers. Mitchell was different. Her background was not merely bookish in some vague way, it was steeped in a specifically British colonial literary tradition of the least critical, most schoolbookish sort. While such a background is by no means confined to the 1950s small town Canada in which she grew up, it certainly differs from the environment of the big American cities where the curriculum was as much American as British and certainly more modernist. Such a colonial, small town mentality characterizes much Canadian writing. Indeed, it would not be difficult to imagine Mitchell, by some caprice, having gone not to art school, but to the University of Toronto, where she likely would have taken classes with Northrop Frye and would surely have spent afternoons in the King Cole Room of the Park Plaza Hotel and contributed much undergraduate verse to *Acta Victoriana*. Before she became an ersatz American, then, Mitchell was, early in her career and probably subconsciously, an ersatz Upper Canadian aesthete, a fact painfully evident now on her first album. At that stage, after all, she knew only two cities — Toronto and Detroit — well. The latter perhaps gave her the first taste of the vicarious decadence she has always craved, but it was the former that provided her with her first mistaken notions of what writers are supposed to be like.

The way in which she divided her first album in twain is but one indication of her self-conscious literariness in those days. The titling of the sections — "I came to the city" and "Out of the city and down to the seaside" — resembles nothing so much as some old narrative poem with the author's synopsis running down the left-hand margin, as in one of those cheap late nineteenth-century editions of "The Rime of the Ancient

Mariner," printed in columns and gaudily bound. She even dedicated the album to her former English teacher, "Mr. Kratzman, who taught me to love words." The lyrics are so highly mannered as to please, no doubt, the old high school instructor whose appreciation of verse must have stopped somewhere short of Rupert Brooke.

At this stage her lyrics were full of outdated images — mermaids, kings, and pirates — that seemed the more dated alongside the contemporary references and the personalized mood of the songs. This mixture of past and present was just as evident, though probably less intentionally so, in the actual production values. For here was a curious situation: David Crosby, who had just left the Byrds, the most sophisticated studio band in Los Angeles, producing a singer whose swooping soprano was the very antithesis of the LA sound. Crosby was forced into making the record distinctive with small touches, such as the use of Stephen Stills on bass in "*Song to a Seagull.*" Another more important Crosby touch was the use of Mitchell's unusual guitar tunings. For a time afterwards, before she first decided to abandon the concert circuit, these tunings were somewhat storied in folk circles. Prior to performances, roadies would place various guitars around the stage, each in a different bizarre tuning, so that Mitchell would not have to interrupt the concert to retune when going from one number to the next. It was often said that the tunings, since they were secret, were part of her success; in truth, any skilled guitarist could have duplicated them from the record with a good ear and a few minutes' experimentation. Yet, significantly, Mitchell appears in retrospect to have actually composed some of the early songs (though not necessarily her most distinctive ones) with these tunings in mind, for the melodies seem written expressly to be so performed.

That first album began Mitchell's career and notoriety, but it was only with the second that many of the characteristics of all her later work appeared in strength. Not that the transition was abrupt. CLOUDS after all was released partly to take advantage of the success of Collins' single of the title song, which was shortly followed by about twenty other covers. CLOUDS also includes "*Chelsea Morning*," another of her literary songs with saccharine lyrics, from 1967:

Woke up, it was a Chelsea morning, and the first
thing that I heard was a song outside
my window, and the

traffic wrote the words. It came ringing up like
Christmas bells, and rapping up like pipes and drums.

But if the album contains some songs she had already outgrown, it also featured some of the small-town sentimentality for which the same could not be said. "*Both Sides Now*," a song she once said was inspired not by a plane trip but by a description of a plane trip in Saul Bellow's *Henderson the Rain King*, is dedicated to her grandmother. Even so, CLOUDS set patterns which still can be found in her work almost as blatantly. Other attitudes, now accepted as part of the Mitchell canon and legend, were just then getting under way.

On CLOUDS, for example, she served as her own producer. She would continue to do so. However, the role played by her long-time sound engineer, Henry Lewy, has gone unstudied, and contributions by mentors along the way probably demand that credit be shared. Also, she did her own cover graphics, as she had done on the first album (whose jacket was psychedelic, apropos nothing much except the spirit of the times) and would usually do henceforth. Also, she again printed her lyrics in full; she was probably the first performer to make an unvarying practice of doing so. More importantly, the second album, the traditional breaking or departure point of so many careers, began in earnest her delight in the autobiography-without-generalization that would soon be so titillating to her audience. "*That Song About the Midway*" and "*The Gallery*" are both said to concern her relationship with Leonard Cohen, with whom she had sometimes been seen, most publicly at the 1967 Newport Folk Festival. All those elements would also be present in LADIES OF THE CANYON, the following album.

In several ways, LADIES OF THE CANYON was the turning point some listeners were awaiting. Here she struggled to pay the penalty for past careerism. Released in 1969, the record includes one song ("*The Circle Game*") written in 1966, which was badly out of place despite all the pre-publicity generated by other hands. A few of the other songs date from 1967 and 1968. The chronology would have been unimportant except that by then Mitchell was so quickly maturing into her distinctive style that these milder, more songwriterish tunes stand out boldly. They clash with the ones created by the artist who seemed to be working arbitrarily in the medium of songwriting.

Also, Mitchell (with her three-octave leaps — like Roy Orbison!) was still engaging in vocal gymnastics as a way of resolving the problem of choppy metrics, in favour of which she dispensed with much of the undergraduate literariness. The result is that she sounds, once or twice, like a telegrapher's key. LADIES OF THE CANYON is such a mixture of new and old elements, such a retelling of her two other albums and a forewarning of her developing legend, that, had she died following its release, it could have been reissued profitably as a combination In Memoriam and Greatest Hits.

The part of the album that previewed what lay ahead is both imaginative and musical. Piano is more prominent now, and cello, flute, clarinet, and baritone sax have been introduced. The writing is just as ambitious. For one thing, from this point one begins to detect that some of the songs written in the first person are fictive, like Gordon Lightfoot's; by 1970 she was so well known that instant recognition forced her even more into being a recluse, and one gets a sense that some of the adventuring had to be conducted in her head. For another, she was not settling into her Tocquevillesque role of trying to pinpoint the spirit of LA, a place which while becoming more familiar still left her with a feeling of untenable foreignness. This is especially evident on the title cut, where she over-enunciates madly, like a drunk trying to compensate for poor diction by giving it greater emphasis. Perhaps the subject matter, lifestyles in upper-middle-class Los Angeles County, left her understandably bewildered even though she followed such lifestyles herself — an anomaly that in some measure is a trait of Californians.

Also on LADIES OF THE CANYON her songs about relationships began to predominate. Of course, she had always been making music from such personal encounters. But when she had been unknown, so had her partners in such passades; now that she was famous, her lovers were her peers. Thus "*Michael from Mountains*" on the first album had been judged only as a song, not as an item in a sexual trade paper, as the same song would have been if Cohen had written it about a person called Michele. By LADIES OF THE CANYON all that changed. The album includes another of the songs ("*Rainy Night House*") said to have been inspired by Cohen. She does indeed seem to be worshipfully emulating, or perhaps merely parodying, Cohen's quasi-religious diction when she writes:

You are a holy man
On the FM radio.

I sat up all night and watched thee
To see, who in the world you might be . . .
You are a refugee
From a wealthy family.
You gave up all the golden factories
To see, who in the world you might be.

But the album was the first in which there were more than one of these emotional post-mortems about other songwriters. "*Willy*," for instance,

*"Mitchell's songs were
often perceived as being
wondrous evocations of
the feminist sensibility."*

was widely taken to be, without protest from its author or apparent subject, a song about Graham Nash. As in the Cohen song, she takes a cool, detached stance, critical not only of her old beau but of herself for having become involved. Indeed, while from the start her music struck responsive chords in thousands of women who felt she almost telepathically intuited and transcribed their own sensations, it was only with LADIES OF THE CANYON that her work included a tincture of feminism. At times this new addition was blatant, as in *"The Arrangement,"* in which, it must be admitted, her concern is with wretches of both sexes, but no less with the one than the other:

> You're the keeper of the cards.
> Yes I know it gets hard
> Keeping the wheels turning,
> And the wife she keeps the keys,
> She is so pleased to be
> A part of the arrangement.
>
> You could have been more
> Than a name on the door
> On the thirty-third floor in the air,
> More than a consumer
> Lying in some room trying to die,
> More than a credit card
> Swimming pool in the backyard . . . .

It is strikingly apparent on the album that, in social as well as personal matters, she is trying to be tougher minded while backing away from such a stand as somehow, in her own mind, too masculine. This, after all, is the album containing *"Woodstock,"* her fey slip into hippie euphoria. This is the most painfully dated of her songs, not because it is about a specific event, the Woodstock festival, but because from the perspective of our time the song reminds many how, like her, they fell for all that commercialized claptrap as having true spiritual significance.

Mitchell, though, always seems far less embarrassed than her listeners at such slips; embarrassment rolls off her back. In reality, perhaps, this is part of her defence. That in the course of one LP she can be both the wounded nocturnal fawn and the cynical bedside chainsmoker; can so earnestly study instant replays of her *affaires* and let pass indiscretions without a wince; can in one song (*"Willy"*) rhyme "blues" and "lose" and in another (*"For Free"*) write an ode to an unknown busker — these are all indications of the way she flits, hummingbird-like, from one enthusiasm to another, one moral stance to the next, one ideology to some other. It is as though she fears stagnating and not being taken seriously if she allows a moment for reflection.

This process is not to be confused with diversity of talent or range of subject. It has more to do with her needing to be perpetually unhappy in her life to be happy with the work that life produces — having experiences *in order that* they affect her adversely. This anomaly mirrors her role in Canadian society. Tied by upbringing to an older culture which has little sympathy with contemporary music, she was proscribed by a later one which questioned her apparent continentalism. She is caught between these two cultural extremes just as she is between the two emotional ones. She throws herself into the life of America so that it can make her unhappy and thus inspire more songs. Joni Mitchell can no more find happiness than Leonard Cohen can find inner peace or Gordon Lightfoot self-confidence; she is the most anguished and hypersensitive of the three.

One of the obvious paths her career took in the all-important 1970s was the process of continuing to rid herself of the preciousness and formal posturing of her early songs. She succeeded to a remarkable extent, even though she still retains the romantic poet's methodology. Almost as common as the notion of her needing a new partner for each album, and with nine records in as many years that bespeaks a quite rapid turnover in personnel, is the sister observation that she also needs fresh geography before setting down to work. Like many linear poets, she produces travel poems to keep herself primed for further work, and sometimes this device comes perilously close to being a crutch. Although perhaps less accurate than the other patent idea about her work habits, it is one that is just as easily proved. BLUE (1971), her final album under the terms of the Reprise contract, demonstrates the point, as well as most of the strengths of her music.

The beginning of the first cut on BLUE virtually serves as a prospectus for her outlook and output as well as setting the scene for what is her only thematic album:

I am on a lonely road and I am travelling
travelling, travelling, travelling
Looking for something, what can it be?
Oh I hate you some, I hate you some
I love you come.
Oh I love you when I forget about me.
I want to be strong, I want to laugh along

I want to belong to the living
Alive, alive, I want to get up and jive
I want to wreck my stockings in some jukebox dive.

These ten lines, which read at first like a satire of fickle soul-bearing, take on another dimension when sung with Mitchell's jagged mellifluousness; they become almost a précis of her past work. They also indicate that on the remainder of the album she will try to extend herself, continue to pursue with clarity the situations alluded to: the almost sado-masochistic relationships in which she plays both parts, with the male a mere catalyst; and the travelling and honkytonking which blur the distinction between actual and vicarious experience. BLUE is the most useful of her albums for study because all her characteristics are in sharp focus and her strengths in full force.

Unlike some of her contemporaries, Mitchell has never been able to maintain for any length of time her best music simultaneously with her best lyric-writing. One or the other usually takes control. On the early records, for instance, the artificially delicate romanticism of the words serves the tunes; later, the melodies become shapeless and at times only reinforce the mood of the lyrics. BLUE remains her finest achievement partly in that the two elements often work as one. By now her melodic phrasing (the result of her struggles in Toronto to find material suited to her vocal range) had become her single most immediately distinctive feature. If sounds themselves could be copyrighted, the style would be Mitchell's property by law, not that infringement would be likely, for by the time of BLUE she had ceased almost entirely being any use to other performers seeking material. They found her songs all but impossible to reproduce in anything like the original manner. Even so, BLUE contains several melodies which, while instantly recognizable as Mitchell, stand out memorably in the context of her work. "*California,*" "*This Flight Tonight,*" and "*River*" could be got up as good instrumentals, a fate ludicrous to contemplate with most of her songs. Again, no producer is listed, but it can be assumed that from this point onwards Mitchell truly began calling her own production shots, with, in this case, a blend of common sense and daring.

Stephen Stills appears on bass and guitar. He is supportive yet unobtrusive, as is James Taylor, who appears on three cuts (doing the same guitar riff on two of them). Taylor's presence repaid a debt owed Mitchell, who had been on his first album, the one produced in England on the Beatles' Apple label before he came to notice in the U.S. and before he and Mitchell worked together on Carole King's famous TAPESTRY. As on several of Mitchell's albums, her nervousness is frequently offset by the confidence and calm of the backup musicians, though at other times just the reverse is true. The production work is notable for taking the dulcimer beyond actual folk music (continuing experiments being carried out by Richard Farina at the time of his death) and for using pedal steel for a kind of imitation-calypso that Mitchell, having toyed with on CLOUDS, was here returning to briefly. Also, the album marks a new cunning in Mitchell's use of piano, which she employs in tinkly cocktail bar fashion to warn of approaching psychic wooziness. Musically, the general impression left by the album is one of slick rock with recurring Latin overtones used for serious artistic ends.

The lyrics are some of Mitchell's most sophisticated and revealing, even though they blend in with the music. Here is Mitchell as the black sheep who, the longer she stays in the United States, the more she discovers incongruities that offset any comforts she knows there. This implication takes several forms, some blatant, some subtle. For example, in *"A Case of You,"* one of the love-hate statements on which BLUE, for the most part, is built, she begins with a passing reference to Canada which, in associating the country with her personal longing, is of more than fleeting importance:

> Just before our love got lost you said
> "I am as constant as a northern star."
> And I said, "Constantly in the darkness,
> Where's that at?
> If you want me I'll be in the bar."
> On the back of a cartoon coaster
> In the blue TV screen light
> I drew a map of Canada
> Oh Canada
> With your face sketched on it twice.

Several elements are at work in these lines. The Canadian reference, one of several throughout the album, shows that she has put Canada behind her and can now remember only the stereotyped images of the country. (The next-to-last line of the above lyric is sung jazz-like to the first bar of *"O Canada."*) She implies, albeit guardedly and only by dint of repetition, that though she is not entirely comfortable in a strange America, neither is she able to return home. She can only draw on memories of the place and time in which life was far less complicated. That is, she is using Canada synonymously with childhood — the idyllic childhood we all occasionally, foolishly concoct for ourselves in our imaginations. She is also showing us her flippant side, the tough-guy cynicism that conflicts with the lovey-dovey declarations of fidelity she often seems to reflect in the choruses to follow. But more important is her sense of being an outsider, which is heightened by generational and class allegiances.

Except at the core, her audience and Leonard Cohen's are not necessarily made up of the same people, but, like Cohen, she is probably older than most of her followers. Again like Cohen, she is undeniably from the middle-class whose values much contemporary music, if it does nothing else, stands foursquare against. Unlike him, however, she does not try to disguise these facts by posing as a saintly ragamuffin. She plays upon them frankly, thus emphasizing her vulnerability. Many of the songs display something akin to discomfort at being at once so popular and so outré. "*California*," for instance, begins with the stanza:

> Sitting in a park in Paris, France
> Reading the news and it sure looks bad;
> They won't give peace a chance,
> That was just a dream some of us had.
> Still a lot of lands to see
> But I wouldn't want to stay here,
> It's too old and cold and settled in its ways here.

The feeling that it is necessary to identify Paris as being in France, lest someone conjure up the image of Paris, Ontario, is an admission of her small-town background. The line is not delivered in the ironic modernist spirit with which Gertrude Stein titled one of her books *Paris France*, to make light of the language of Midwest rubbernecks who followed the serious expatriates of the 1920s. Mitchell's rather cavalier sighing about the failure of the peace movement (perhaps the only overtly political statement in any of her songs for years to come) is also typical of her outcast stance. On socio-political questions she speaks out on both sides, as though uncertain on which she belongs. The peace movement was an essentially American phenomenon — fittingly enough, since the war in question was an American war. It sprang from a century of American radical tradition, more cultural than political between about 1940 and 1964 but unbroken all the same, rather than from the 1950s movement for nuclear-disarmament that was largely British and European in impetus. One could not usefully check into it, as though into a hotel. Mitchell sensed clearly that, while her sympathies were in the right place and were certainly fashionable at the time, her understanding was oblique. Her political viewpoint on the question of the war was that of a foreign national.

The bridge of "*California*" goes like this:

Oh, but California
California, I'm coming home
I'm going to see the folks I dig
I'll even kiss a Sunset pig
California I'm coming home.

But the enthusiasm is as forced as the slang, which even then (1971) was dated. The inference to be drawn is that, because its loneliness is at least familiar, California is home, now that Canada has changed so much in her absence. The point is not that the one is home and the other a temporary domicile, but that she is not truly comfortable in either. California is a base of operations; Canada the source of both the adolescent memories which haunt her and the contradictions and inconsistencies which characterize her. The one is the home to which she cannot return; the other the place from which she cannot proceed. This sense of being in limbo, which is perhaps lost on some of her U.S. following, is clear enough from a Canadian perspective. It meshes nicely with the romantic ups and downs so central to her diarist's approach. Indeed, the one is a good metaphor for the other. But then BLUE is an album full of helpful metaphors and illuminating revelations.

In "*The Last Time I Saw Richard*" she describes a reunion with a former lover who, on the evidence of the song, sounds like the exact male opposite of Mitchell herself in one of her romantic moods. Perhaps that accounts for the tone of slightly veiled contempt, the product of her other, equally extreme unromantic side:

The last time I saw Richard was Detroit in '68
And he told me all romantics meet the same fate someday
Cynical and drunk and boring someone in some dark café.
"You laugh," he said. "You think you're immune.
Go look at your eyes, they're full of moon.
You like roses and kisses and pretty men to tell you
All those pretty lies, pretty lies.
Only pretty lies, just pretty lies."

The song shows not only that she can work with incredibly long lines, but that by 1971 the diary songs were sometimes as much a crutch as the travel songs. Mitchell gets the penultimate laugh in the relationship by pointing out that:

> Richard got married to a figure skater,
> And he bought her a dishwasher and a coffee percolator
> And he drinks at home most nights with the TV on . . . .

But the effect rings hollow. This, the last cut on the album, lingers in the careful listener's memory because it is clear that, based on what Mitchell has told us in dozens of songs, Richard, whoever he was or is, was undeniably correct in his assessment of her. Richard himself had the last laugh since he at least found a place which, however kitschy, is home.

All during the 1970s, and especially after the release of BLUE, Mitchell was closely identified with Los Angeles music — not just with the characteristic sound as it has developed through successive waves of fashion, but with the process of creating and shaping that sound in studio. Session musicians have become fashionable by working with her. That is curious in view of the fact that her switch to the Asylum label in 1972 had relatively little effect on the course of her work. Instead, her music has continued to spring from the tensions within herself as a writer — between a sense of familiarity and her sense of being an outsider; between aggressive statements and passive roles; between romanticism and jaded nightclub cynicism. Seldom do musical sparks leap between herself and the others with whom she surrounds herself in the studio; the albums are Mitchell productions from first to last despite all the expensive talent she gathers around her.

Her initial album for the Asylum label, FOR THE ROSES, was recorded at A & M studios in Hollywood, a place that often left a distinctive mark, especially on artists newly arrived there. Phil Ochs, for example, was orchestrated to some profit but almost beyond recognition when he first recorded there after leaving Elektra. In Mitchell's case there are no such signs; in fact, she seems almost to have purposefully resisted the threat of such influence. The album uses strings and woodwinds, but their effect is countered by her reliance on old friends and standbys such as Stills and (on harmonica) Graham Nash. Again, she was her own producer, with acknowledged "guidance" from Henry Lewy. Her doggedness in this matter helped make the resulting record one characterized by simple melodies and downcast, almost self-pitying lyrics. Only one of the songs, *"You Turn Me On (I'm a Radio),"* shows anything other than the depressive aspect of her manic-depressive recorded personality, and it was a

"Joni Mitchell can no more find happiness than Leonard Cohen can find inner peace or Gordon Lightfoot self-confidence."

successful single. But despite that bit of whimsy, the album is remarkable for casual and self-indulgent writing, leaning more towards disconnected imagery than earlier records, thus increasing the melancholy. There are, however, one or two signs of her knack at summing up a mood, as in "*Banquet*," a song somewhat influenced by Cohen:

> Some turn to Jesus
> and some to heroin
> Some turn to rambling
> looking for a clear sky
> and drinking stream.
> Some watch the paint peel off
> Some watch their kids grow up
> Some watch their stocks and bonds
> waiting for that big deal
> American dream.

It was her most intensely personal album up to that time and perhaps the most intimate of them all. As a consequence, it is the one most blatant about her childhood and its effects, and thus about her misty, bittersweet conception of Canada. In "*Let the Wind Carry Me*," for instance, she is at pains to show that, whatever Canada and youth have become in her adult imagination, she was in reality just as out of place then as she is in present-day America:

> Papa's faith is people,
> Mamma she believes in cleaning . . .
> Papa brought home the sugar
> Mamma taught me the deeper meaning
> She don't like my kick-pleat skirt
> She don't like my eyelids painted green
> She don't like my staying up late
> in my high-heeled shoes
> living for that rock 'n' roll dancing scene . . .
> Mamma thinks she spoilt me
> Papa knows he set me free . . .
> Sometimes I get that feeling
> and want to settle
> and raise a child with somebody
> I get that strong longing . . .
> but it passes like the summer.

I'm a wild seed again
Let the wind carry me.

Elsewhere, in "*Lesson in Survival*," she describes a personal relationship in such a way as to make what seems, from a Canadian viewpoint, a further statement on her inability to be bi-national:

Maybe it's paranoia
Maybe it's sensitivity
Your friends protect you
scrutinize me.
I get so damn timid,
not at all the spirit
that's inside of me.

Because it is one of her least experimental and hence more natural albums, FOR THE ROSES is also her most doleful. And it was perhaps her least successful critically. The second Asylum LP, however, was the opposite in every respect. COURT AND SPARK, released in 1974, was almost as diverse musically as THE HISSING OF THE SUMMER LAWNS one year later, and was also a critical and financial hit, though its success probably had something to do with almost atavistic regression. In FOR THE ROSES, Mitchell at least had held a consistent viewpoint, albeit a rather unattractive one, and the audience had responded with less than universal enthusiasm. Such consistency had not only increased her tendency towards melodic sameness, it had also deprived her of the rapid emotional climbs and shattering plummets (so like the vocal highs and lows she struggled with), thus confirming the image of her held by her detractors while disappointing her champions.

If Mitchell were known to be calculating, it would be tempting to state that she planned COURT AND SPARK in an attempt to regain her popularity. It is an amazing album in that it seems to be trying to please everyone. There are several of the romantically equivocal songs one would expect but also a few superficial ones and at least one, "*Free Man in Paris*," that fits neither category. This song is an example of her songwriting at its purest — unadorned without being primitive, forceful not forced. Taken as a single unit, however, the album is notable because it features one of the largest and most improbable accumulations of side men in contemporary music, with David Crosby, Graham Nash, Robbie Robertson, Jose Feliciano, and Tom Scott, among others. Also, and not coincidentally, this is the one album most influenced by other musicians.

Of the various strains evident on COURT AND SPARK, the most obvious is jazz. From the start Mitchell has been most important as a separate musical entity rather than as part of any long-range musical trend. But she has always been secondarily important as a kind of clearing house of musical ideas. The success of her singular style (and it has become more individualistic with the years) has not kept her from continuing to absorb influences and let them loose on a public that has, in turn, felt their attraction second hand. Both musicians and certain lyricists have influenced her writing; the former more notably so. Crosby, Stills and Nash undoubtedly have been among the primary melodic and structural influences on her work, both singly and as a group. Crosby's first solo album, for instance, still echoes in some of her songs. Significantly, they are among the few groups in the genre who understand something of jazz. And while Mitchell's musical diction owes something to Jackson Browne, she also has much in common in this area with Bruce Cockburn. Both she and Cockburn, for example, look to jazz to bolster their folksy lines and are at least academically interested in jazz guitar. On COURT AND SPARK, Mitchell used jazz guitar to signal cues, but this may well have been a result of Tom Scott's presence, which has been insufficiently recognized. Scott was the leader of the group LA Express and plays sax and all the reeds. He did some of the arrangements on the albums and later, when Mitchell returned to concerts on the record's success, was on the road with her intermittently for seven months. The mark he left on her both in studio and in concert is evident on her only live album, MILES OF AISLES (1974). It is most direct, however, on COURT AND SPARK in many general ways relating to jazz.

Much has been made of Mitchell's links to jazz, but it is a question to which there are two sides. Her voice does have a quirky flavour suggestive of jazz. Later she began developing even more an improvisational tone in her singing. But the fact that she doesn't write songs in studio and even prints all her lyrics in full would argue against its importance. Ultimately, she lacks the jazz singer's particular sense of rhythm, even though she comes nearer to possessing it than anyone else with folk roots. The result is that she uses jazz in a folky way, and rather ingeniously and honestly at that. Some jazz men, George Benson for one, incorporated rock into their jazz to keep their audiences from dwindling; but they increasingly skimped on the jazz and become more and more men of rock. Conversely, Mitchell has worked jazz into her folk but without necessarily watering down either. Perhaps that is one of the lessons learned from Scott, who also in his merging of jazz and rock came close to satisfying devotees of both forms.

COURT AND SPARK (the title seems to mock an earlier phase in the progress of her sensibility) has one other distinction in this regard. The album marked the first occasion when she recorded a song written by someone else, "*Twisted*," the jazz standard first recorded in 1951 by the English jazz singer Annie Ross. "*Twisted*" has a curious history. The melody was written by Wardell Grey, the tenor saxophonist who died in the desert near Las Vegas under mysterious circumstances. Ross, a drug addict who kicked the habit only to be rehooked by Lenny Bruce, added the first-person lyric in which, Captain Queeg-like, a psychotic makes plain her disturbance while professing sanity. Her rendering of it made fashionable the style of singing called vocalese, which presupposes an impressive vocal range, though vocalese was first used by King Pleasure and there are other examples just as good, such as James Moody's "*Mood of Love*" and the SING A SONG OF BASIE record by Ross, Dave Lambert, and Jon Hendricks. It is significant that on the first occasion she dipped into jazz history, Mitchell did so with such an accessible and prominent number, one which in its vocal style and emotional extremes resembled her original work and made clear what she doubtless considered the connection between them.

This experiment of reaching back into other types of music continued and all but got out of hand on THE HISSING OF THE SUMMER LAWNS, which followed MILES OF AISLES in autumn 1975. On that album her new interest in jazz, as a means of continuing to quiet her fears about being the poor man's Joan Baez, is even more prominent. So are the alternating mellowness and aggressiveness of the lyrics. Together, the two elements bring on a lack of direction, and the album was greeted with some disappointment. The greatest innovation and the rarest occurrence in terms of Mitchell's career came in her notes to the album rather than on the record itself. The notes, in tone so reminiscent of Leonard Cohen's, are as close as she has come to assessing or explaining any of her work:

> This record is a total work conceived graphically, musically, lyrically and accidentally — as a whole. The performances were guided by the given compositional structures and the audibly inspired beauty of every player. The whole unfolded like a mystery. It is not my intention to unravel that mystery for anyone, but rather to offer some additional clues. "*Centerpiece*" is a Johnny Mandel-Jon Hendricks tune. John Guerin and I collaborated on "*The Hissing of Summer Lawns*." "*The Boho Dance*" is a Tom Wolfe-ism from the book *The Painted Word*. "*Don't Interrupt the Sorrow*" was born around 4 a.m.

in a New York loft. Larry Poons seeded it and Bobby Neuwirth was midwife here, but the child filtered through Genesis at Jackfish Lake, Saskatchewan, is rebellious and mystical and insists that its conception was immaculate . . . I would especially like to thank Myrt and Bill Anderson, North Battleford, New York, Saskatoon, Bel-Air, Burbank, Burundi, Orange County, the deep deep heart of Dixie, Blue, *National Geographic Magazine*, Helpful Henry the Housewife's Delight — and John Guerin for showing me the root of the chord and where I was.

That last bit of self-depreciation (again, reminiscent of Cohen) can almost be read as punch-pulling, a bit of humility to counter the earlier catalogue of narcissism, a narcissism that has always been as much a part of her image as vulnerability and cynicism and perhaps even more of a front. Considering her records as products, for example, without actually listening to them, would give one a distorted impression of the personality inside. She would appear to be inordinately self-absorbed. Her own artwork decorates most of her albums. She long used large photographs of herself that became progressively more daring and artificial, a practice that climaxed in the arty nude study (from the rear, facing the ocean) concealed on the interior flap of FOR THE ROSES. The spectacle of her own body (there are other examples) later gave way to photos in which she tried desperately to look chic and sophisticated and at the same time intellectual. This last attitude has come relatively late, as evidenced by the above liner note, and by HEJIRA, released late in 1976.

To all outward appearances HEJIRA is her most Los Angeles album. Percussion, bass, and vibes are used in the characteristic LA manner. Even the jacket (her own design again) seeks to be very West Coast. It shows her in a fur coat and beret, smoking a cigarette (as she often is in posed photographs and as indeed she must have been during the sessions, judging by her shortness of breath on some of the cuts). She looks, on this cover, like someone who was married to Man Ray, circa 1936. Her face is the main component of a politely surreal collage that is bohemianism elevated to the level of trendy, intellectual sophistication — Wilshire Boulevard's notion of the Boul Mich. All such details, down to the deviant spelling of *hegira*, make her case, but the songs themselves contradict it. Her voice remains too birdlike to be LA incarnate and her interest in jazz, formerly so studio inspired, here mushrooms into a quite distinctive lyric trait.

But if it lacks the diversity of BLUE and the concentration of LADIES OF

THE CANYON, HEJIRA does contain many of the finest lyrics Mitchell has ever written. Some are so tight and measured that in the hands of someone else (Leonard Cohen or perhaps Loudon Wainwright) they would tend to suggest their own melodies:

> I'm travelling in some vehicle
> I'm sitting in some café
> A defector from the pretty wars
> That shellshock love away.
> There's comfort in melancholy
> When there's no need to explain.
> It's just as natural as the weather
> In this moody sky today.

Mitchell, though, does not allow them to take control. She fits them into melodic lines that test her great skill at phrasing. As before, she bunches, stretches, and condenses phrases in unusual ways, somewhat like a projectivist poet expert at breath control. Here, however, she often does so with quite long lines that simply have more syllables in them than those in most of her older songs (excepting "*The Last Time I Saw Richard*") and are therefore more difficult to bend into shape. The lyrics give a bit, the melodies give a bit, and the total effect is as much jazz-like as that of her more recognizably jazz-inspired songs. It is indeed as though she is at times using her voice as another instrument; but in fact she is creating an almost contrapuntal relationship between melody and lyric without abandoning the line of descent from folk.

Each Mitchell album has contained a few surprises. LADIES OF THE CANYON slipped first into calypso and then into actual rock 'n' roll with "*Big Yellow Taxi*." On FOR THE ROSES she used four-letter words at odds with what otherwise was her ladylike diction. In HEJIRA the surprises come both in the lyrics and the music. There is one song about her sense of being the outsider during a visit to the old Memphis bluesman Furry Lewis:

> W.C. Handy I'm rich and I'm fey
> And I'm not that familiar with what you played,
> But I get such strong impressions of your heyday
> Looking up and down old Beale Street.
> Ghosts of darktown society
> Come right out of the bricks at me.
> Like it's Saturday night
> They're in their finery

Dancing it up and making deals.
Furry sings the blues.

Logically, the song is written as an imitation blues, but the production bogs down, only partly because of the harmonica work by Neil Young, who joins John Guerin and a largely new cast of studio musicians. A bigger and more successful surprise is *"Blue Motel Room"* which, true to her eclecticism but striking all the same, is an old fashioned, slit-skirt, reclining-on-the-piano torch song, such as might have been written for an early Lauren Bacall movie. The wonder is that Mitchell never came around to writing such a piece earlier, though the surprise element is that the cut confirms musically a change also evident in the lyric of another song, *"A Strange Boy"*: that, much to her amazement and sorrow, she is getting older while her constant search of belonging becomes more desperate. Only with *"A Strange Boy"* do her songs about lovers and loving take a fresh turn. As the title suggests and as the lyric explains at some length, the song is about someone much younger than herself, a fact that adds a new dimension to the note of disappointment running through her work. The song seems to say that, at thirty-three, Mitchell found herself in the role of the Older Woman. And that is very Los Angeles, very American, very everything that has both attracted and repelled her since she left Canada so long ago.

What can be said for Mitchell at such a stage in her creative life, and what, if anything, does it have to do with her having been raised in Canada? Coming at the tail end of the folk movement, she was forced by circumstances to seek new directions. She succeeded where many others, like silent film stars in the new age of talkies, failed. She has continued evolving in a way that has been unique if not always smooth. She has not rested on her achievements but has always been willing (despite the veneer of egotism) to try new things musically, and sometimes lyrically as well.

Although she wrote in *"For Free"* on LADIES OF THE CANYON that she pursues her career "for fortune and those velvet curtain calls," she has forsaken live performances for far longer periods than she has embraced them. Even when she does perform in concert, she is capable of incredible bursts of nervousness and stage fright amid engagements otherwise distinguished by fluency and easy grace. The same kind of nervousness is present at her recording sessions. While this behaviour is, in itself, no indication of nationality, it is a sign that like Lightfoot and Cohen, she is neither a concert performer nor a recording artist foremost. Despite what seems her elaborate studio technique, her recent LPs have perpetuated the aural strategy credited to Sandy Perleman on Bob Dylan's BLONDE ON

BLONDE, namely, an indifference to the way the finished product sounds in stereo and an almost ideological disregard for orchestration as a process. There is little doubt that Mitchell is primarily a writer; and not just a writer, but one whose influence, though indirect, has been immense.

Although the proposition was never quite articulated publicly, there long existed the notion that the type of personal art music left by the folk movement came in two genders: Male Songs, which were often unimportant statements of something tangible; and Female Songs, important statements on subjects too emotionally fragile and abstract for naming. Mitchell

"Mitchell epitomized and indeed helped shape the mood of the late 1970s."

helped dismantle that idea and make respectable songs which, taken together, illustrate the search for fulfilment whatever the writer's sex. She thereby expanded on the revolutionary process begun by Dylan of making the creator more important than the merchant. In so doing, she also helped to legitimize what was once dismissed as the so-called album song. In her way, and mainly by example, she has contributed to the revitalization, improvement, and expression of a tradition of songwriting that was mainly European in origin and once closely associated with cabarets. If she has unwittingly encouraged Dory Prévin, she has also made possible the further development of Maria Muldar, Carly Simon, Janis Ian, and a score of others who slowly came to the kind of quiet, dignified despair one would have expected to find in a young Edith Piaf.

More important, but far less easy to describe, is her place outside the music industry, in the whole society as it regards both men and women. Here again her cultural background comes into play, tinged with elements she would have been heir to had she remained in Canada. In expressing herself from the, at times, unconscious position of the outsider and the black sheep, she has given voice to old reticence while also struggling for the sometimes strident outspokenness. The result has been frankness about her personal life interspersed with a turning away from such candour. It is as though she is shocking herself; as though she wishes to continue being docile and feminine in the old way while also being the equal and even superior partner in any enterprise; as though, like Groucho Marx, she refuses to join any club that would condescend to have her as a member. There is a line on BLUE about "reading *Rolling Stone*, reading *Vogue*" that goes a long way towards describing this phenomenon. She tries to belong to the audience of both those publications but ends being only an interloper in each. She can write of her wardrobe and her riches and her hankering for sophistication with one hand, then with the other write about Woodstock. That she fails to convince even herself of her total sympathy creates a deep rapport with her audience, which is in somewhat the same position.

Her audience was gestated in the 1960s, a period of extremes. Coming from a background that is less extreme, she fits in better during the morning after than she would have at the party the night before. Her American audience spent the 1960s searching for hipness in reaction to everything their parents told them, most of which turned out to be incorrect anyway, but which at least had the advantage of representing some sort of system of values to which they were tied. They began believing that hip was remaining aloof to such values; later they saw hipness in mocking themselves and their former reserve. The way "dope" and "freak," cant words of their parents' generation, came back into use as simple nouns without pejorative overtones, is one random example of this change; another might be the revival of interest in hip 1970s circles of all the television pap (*Leave it to Beaver, Mickey Mouse Club, Howdy Doody*) which they had wasted their childhood days innocently watching. Suddenly hip was to be found in the distance one had travelled without forgetting whence one had come. Slowly it came to be equated with self-evaluation in the present without much reference to pop culture. Once an affectation, later an attitude, it finally became a state of mind.

Mitchell fitted perfectly in such a scheme of things. Both as a writer and as a person written about, she came to be seen as one who shares her foibles and misgivings, her periods of seeming happiness and self-doubt. Mitchell epitomized and indeed helped shape the mood of the late 1970s, in which the thought dawned that maybe hip does not really exist except in relation to oneself, or that if it does, it does not lie solely in acting cool and coy to keep from being gauche and embarrassed.

There's a line on Kris Kristofferson's album SURREAL THING calculated to evoke squeamishness on the part of the modern-day listener: "Hearin' Joni Mitchell is better than smokin' grass." Admittedly it sounds even more asinine out of context, but the sentiment is one that Mitchell herself could well have written about someone else, in which case it would have been applauded as self-discovery. For that is what she is selling. The emotional journal she started out writing in the 1960s is still being compiled and sung. Yet she has long since ceased being that quintessential 1960s and 1970s type, the singer-songwriter. From time to time younger figures such as Suzanne Vega appear whose debt to her is to a Mitchell who no longer exists; others, however, Canadians especially, including figures as different as Jane Siberry, Connie Kaldar, and Rita MacNeil, acknowledge a different Mitchell, the one who seems to be open to so many distinct forms of music, from folk to rock and pop to jazz. But what seems to them to be her example of infinite choice may have become a prison to Mitchell herself. In the late 1970s she inclined more and more towards jazz. She reached something like the jazz ideal of co-ordinated improvisational ecstasy on her double album, DON JUAN'S RECKLESS DAUGHTER (1977), working with a group of musicians that included the bassist Jaco Pastorius and the drummer and percussionist Don Alias (what a name for a jazz man). She tried to carry on in that vein with MINGUS, a studio album in collaboration with the legendary bassist and composer Charlie Mingus, only to draw back in the next one, WILD THINGS RUN FAST, in 1982. Thus was the pattern established. Since then, she has been bouncing from jazz to rock, as though to mirror the way her songs ricochet from one emotional extreme to the other. Jazz has been music into which she has retreated in order to escape rock (and vice versa). It is worth asking, however, just what her commitment to it is.

This is dangerous ground. Jazz after all was the art that proved criticism worthless as a shaping influence. Yet it seems perfectly fair to make several remarks. The main attraction of the modern jazz idiom is that its elasticity fit her growing musical knowledge, but at the same time her use of jazz shows up her weaknesses as a producer, especially on her albums with Geffen Records (the label formed by David Geffen, who had risen from the mailroom of the William Morris Agency to start Asylum Records and managed the careers of, among others, Jackson Browne, Laura Nyro, and Crosby Stills Nash & Young). When she chooses to be, she is indeed a genuine jazz singer, with horn phrasing and the like.

Another point to consider is that, with jazz, Mitchell could continue to pursue what she had begun to experiment with in that rooming house on Huron Street in Toronto, writing music suited to her extraordinary vocal range. Her sound is defined by her great range just as Leonard Cohen's sound is defined by his lack of range. In much of her later music, the uses to which she puts her voice bring to mind what civil engineers call "hunting behaviour," the process by which a suspension bridge, for example, will oscillate in a storm until it locates the position at which it can accommodate the stress. All of the above, however, have had the negative effect of giving her jazz-influenced recordings a sense of sterility. After all, she is not coming to jazz from any solid historic perspective. Kenneth Rexroth once remarked that Black musicians in America moved towards jazz inexorably, inevitably, for the same reason that Russian novelists embraced metaphysics following the failed revolution of 1905: it was a language the cops didn't understand. That certainly isn't the case with Mitchell. It's only by being Canadian, a culturally exploited but hardly an *oppressed* minority, that she qualifies as an outsider. She simply uses jazz as a mark of sophistication in an aural collage that includes vernacular and pop-culture elements as well. The process is obvious in her three albums from the 1980s.

WILD THINGS RUN FAST (1982) withdrew to her previous position and let rock elements dominate the jazz ones, and matched the two sounds with two different emotional stances: sloppy sentiment and sophisticated *hateur.* In *"Chinese Cafe"* she sings about a nostalgic visit to the Prairies, where she recognizes her own condition in old childhood friends who are now themselves "middle class, middle-aged." In *"Solid Live"* she can mourn the effectiveness of "love bandits"; in another cut, *"Love,"* she can soliloquize about falling in love, being in love, having loved. "When I became a woman I put away childish things," she says hopefully. Well, no, not quite. Such mush coexists happily with "*Be Cool*," in which she exhorts people to "play it cool, fifty-fifty fire and ice." In "*Man to Man*" she plays into the old stereotype of herself by admitting "Lots of guys go through my door," by asking "How come I keep movin' from man to man?" Such a song (written before she married the bassist Larry Klein) would have been daring coming from a far younger Mitchell, still trying to shock the folks back in Saskatoon. What does it mean coming from the present one? An answer appears in recognizing that on this album, as on DOG EAT DOG (1985) and CHALK MARKS IN A RAIN STORM (1988), there are musical references to the pop culture of the late 1950s and early 1960s, a few bars here, a few bars there, like the clues in some radio station's nostalgia contest.

After the jazz elements in WILD THINGS were greeted with critical calumny, Mitchell switched managers, taking up with Peter Asher, and took off in a queer new way. DOG EAT DOG was not just a pulling away from jazz but a swing in a different direction, combining electronic music with songs of protest. Never had a synthesizer been used for such purposes, to enhance songs lashing out against evangelists, chemical fertilizers, the media, the nuclear arms race, and cigarette consumption. The total effect was like one of those well-rounded nineteenth-century radicals for whom vegetarianism and decimal coinage for the British empire were parts of the same overall cause, though at times the listener might more easily have been reminded of Phil Ochs, desperately searching for wrongs to right in order to fill up an album in 1964 or 1965 — except that in Mitchell's case there was more sermonizing than journalizing.

On one cut, significantly, she remarks of America that she can never "stay here long enough to really understand" the inherent craziness of its culture. There is a desperation in that line matching the desperation in her later career, with its quick embrace of one style, one approach (on rare occasions you might say one gimmick), only to discard it for another. CHALK MARK IN A RAIN STORM kept a bit of the synthesizer, for instance, and a bit of the protest as well, with songs in support of Native land claims and Vietnam War veterans. But its prevailing device was the use of an unusual cast of guest performers, some of them in conventional duets, others playing assigned roles in the total mix. Billy Idol, Tom Petty, and Peter Gabriel were some of these co-conspirators. Another was Willie Nelson, with whom she sings in close harmony on a version of "*Cool, Cool Water.*" Collaboration with Willie Nelson is always a sign of a musical career in panicky transition.

Through it all, Mitchell, in her niche in the culture, has come to take on some of the terrifying characteristics we associate with rich, famous, and important widows, like Jacqueline Kennedy Onassis or Yoko Ono or, in previous times, Madame Chiang Kai-Shek, the sort of public personality you don't want to mess with, yet are fascinated by. She has been at it a sufficiently long time, through so many different eras of popular music, including a few which she herself has helped to open or close, that a certain sense of history clings to her. Some find that comforting, others terrifying.

four

ROBBIE ROBERTSON
The Guilt of Being in Demand

"Robertson is a fervent believer in using modern music to bring history to the public."

On November 25, 1976, Thanksgiving Day in the United States, five thousand people who had paid twenty-five dollars each filled the Winterland auditorium in San Francisco to see the Band in what was billed as their final concert — The Last Waltz. The hall had been decorated with fake Greek and Roman statuary on loan from Twentieth Century-Fox and with backdrops borrowed from the San Francisco Opera Company's production of *La Traviata*. Six huge chandeliers, designed for *Gone With the Wind*, hung from the ceiling. While a chamber group played Viennese waltzes, the audience was treated to a sit-down dinner consisting of two and three-quarter tons of turkey with ninety gallons of gravy, five hundred pounds of onions, three hundred and fifty pounds of croutons and two hundred and fifty pounds of butter. There were also six thousand bread rolls, a ton of yams, and four hundred gallons of apple juice. In a generous move, Bob Dylan had ordered three hundred pounds of Nova Scotia salmon flown in from New York.

The whole affair was promoted and managed by Bill Graham, and after the meal some of his five-hundred-and-eighteen-man staff removed the tables so the show could begin. The concert included guest appearances by Joni Mitchell, Neil Young, Eric Clapton, Van Morrison, Paul Butterfield, Dr. John and Ringo Starr. Ronnie Hawkins, who had originally put together this group of four Canadians (Robbie Robertson, Garth Hudson, Rick Danko, Richard Manuel) and one American (Levon Helm), also played. So of course did Dylan, who had taken them out of such relative obscurity and put them in a position to be recognized as one of the most influential rock bands ever assembled. The show lasted four hours, not counting the opening feast or the long party afterwards. It included a new song, *"Last Waltz,"* written for the occasion by Robbie Robertson, whom Greil Marcus once called the group's "lyricist, manager, strategist, savant, visionary and spokesman."

Everywhere there was a feeling The Last Waltz was a musical event of intimidating significance. This sense came not merely from the fact that Martin Scorsese, who had paid a $100,000 advance for film rights, was wandering the hall with a camera crew, nor from the fact that the performances would be put in permanent form on a commemorative album, but from the fact that this gathering summarized much of rock history. If not so apt a sociological symbol as Woodstock, it was at least part of the parade of events that stretched from the 1965 Newport Folk Festival, when Dylan had been booed for introducing his electric sound, to Watkins Glen in 1973, when an audience of six hundred thousand (the largest ever assembled for a concert up to that time) had shown rock's true magnitude. Both were events in which the Band, or some of it, had participated. The Last Waltz was the end of an era, for better as well as for worse, and the event glowed with a certain symmetry and appropriateness. The Last Waltz was being held in the same building in which the musicians, six years earlier, had given their first concert as the Band, the latest, and as it happened, last, of many incarnations its various members had lived. The event fell eight years after their first album together and twelve after their meeting up with Dylan. But it also made clear that the roots of the Band extended back still farther. Held, after all, on Thanksgiving (a typically religious gesture for a group subconsciously concerned with spiritual matters), it was an act of thanksgiving on a grand scale for a long career together, longer than the Beatles', longer than the Rolling Stones' up to that time; a career that, though its chronology is often difficult to unravel, covers practically the entire span of rock 'n' roll from its rise to its flowering as a tribal activity and its ultimate emergence as a source of individual expression; a career that while tied to Canada in important and sometimes subtle ways, received its impetus on two occasions from Americans, Ronnie Hawkins and Bob Dylan.

Hawkins is as much a legendary figure in Canadian music as anyone. Part of his legend has been that he was even a legendary figure in the United States before moving to Toronto in 1958, though like much folklore, this is not necessarily borne out by a cold examination of the facts. A native of Hawkins Holler in the Ozark Mountains of Arkansas, he was nonetheless raised in a prosperous middle-class family and well educated. He has claimed to have recorded the first ever rock 'n' roll single, in 1952, but as one critic has pointed out, discographers have yet to locate any trace of it. He did make the charts twice in the late 1950s with one of his own songs, "*Mary Lou*," and with a cover of Chuck Berry's "*Forty Days*," but the evidence shows him to have been anything but the star many Canadian writers on the subject have claimed he was. His was one of many countrified rock 'n' roll acts playing the southern roadhouses and juke joints and making inroads into Canada during the fallow seasons, which might come at any moment and last any length of time.

Such groups tended to sound alike since their repertoires were likely to consist of whatever was on the jukeboxes at the moment. The sameness was heightened by a volatility of personnel for which such bands were notorious. Hawkins' outfit, the Hawks, was no exception. The first of what would eventually be important additions came with Levon Helm, a drummer from Marvel, Arkansas, who headed a group called the Jungle Bush Beaters. Shortly before Hawkins immigrated to Canada, Helm chanced to be booked with Hawkins and the Hawks and was impressed with their rockabilly style; he joined the next day. Times were rough, and Helm went with his new leader to Canada, where the country audiences were just as eager as in the U.S. but where rockers with some claim to authentic white-trash roots were considerably fewer and more in demand. In Ontario the group catered to that massive native audience for country music, which because it has had little access to the urban Canadian media has tended to be ignored for long periods. They catered, that is, to the Canadian working class that makes up such a disproportionately large share of the audience at any convocation of the Grand Ole Opry or the WWVA Jamboree — which is not to say that life was easier, only that it was easier to get noticed. The group got its first important recording contract with Roulette Records, a minor American label, after being spotted by an A&R man in a Hamilton bar during the kind of gig that was good work but not always to be had. In 1959 the original Hawks began to drift away, to be replaced by people who together with Helm would eventually, as much in humility as in arrogance, call themselves *the* Band, as though there were no other.

The exact order of who-joined-when is not always clear, in common with much early detail about this group, one so essentially musical as to eclipse such linear considerations. Suffice it to say that the vacancies in the Hawks were filled by people recruited from local bands around Toronto and that eventually the newcomers joined Helm in departing Hawkins to play as Levon and the Hawks. Richard Manuel, from Stratford, signed on as vocalist and piano pounder. The least impressive solo artist but an integral part of the whole, he came from a group named the Revols, a shortened form of Revolutions. Garth Hudson came from London, Ontario, and incidentally is the most Canadian *looking* of the lot; with his domed forehead and a beard that looks as though it should hook behind his ears with wire, he resembles some character in a James Reaney play. He arrived from a group called Paul London and the Capters (not Captors nor Copters but *Capters*), joined Hawkins in Toronto, toured with him in the United States and returned to Toronto in 1962 to be with Levon and the Hawks as organist. Rick Danko, who had begun playing accordion at ethnic weddings around Delhi, Ontario, where he grew up, became the Hawks' bassist. Finally and most importantly there was Jamie Robbie Robertson (he dropped the first name about 1971). Born in Toronto in 1943, he left school to play with a group called the Robots; later he was involved with the Consuls and with Thumper and the Trombones, groups equally deserving of obscurity. He joined Hawkins as a replacement for Fred Carter, one of the guitarists who influenced his style, though not to the same extent as did Roy Buchanan ("the best unknown guitarist in the world") who was then playing with Dale Hawkins, Ronnie's cousin. Robertson was sixteen, by which time (accounts vary) he had already worked one or two years writing songs, two of which Hawkins recorded.

Hawkins ran a tight show but a wearying one. In their years with him, Helm, Danko, Hudson, Manuel, and Robertson toured southern Ontario and the sleazy spots of the South, playing six or seven nights a week, fifty-one weeks a year. They performed regularly, as Hudson would recall, "for pimps, rounders and flakeouts." They rode in Hawkins' Cadillac, pulling their instruments and sound system behind them in a small trailer. After approximately three years of this life, they continued to tour the U.S. but as the Canadian Squires, under which name they recorded another of Robertson's early songs, "*The Stones I Throw*," without much success. For the most part, though, they played home territory, mainly as Levon and the Hawks, but for a time as the Crackers, a name they later revived as an inside joke. It was as the Hawks, however, that they achieved a level of perfection and degree of integration which brought them renown as perhaps the most memorable of all Yonge Street bar bands, a distinction that would be very important to their later life together.

During those years, the early and middle 1960s, the musical climate was changing once more. Rock 'n' roll was becoming less a matter of formula and cheap choreography; rock 'n' roll was becoming plain rock. In Toronto, this meant that a different kind of music was rising in a new setting just as folk and the Yorkville coffee houses were starting their decline. Taverns on the Yonge Street strip, such as the Edison, Steeles, Le Coq d'Or, the Nickelodeon, and the Zanzibar, gave rise to the Canadian bar bands and also to a certain subculture, whose members included persons like Cathy Evelyn Smith, who would serve time in prison for administering a fatal drug overdose to John Belushi in 1982. For a time, Toronto, like Memphis, would appear to have a distinctive style of such music, though for a different reason. In Memphis, as in Nashville, the bands were made up of aspiring country musicians who migrated there hoping to make it big. Toronto's sound had more to do with the history of the city and the nature of the bars themselves.

There is no more characteristically Canadian institution than the beer parlour, with its uncomfortable chairs, minimalist decoration, and beer of indistinguishable brand slopped down on bare tables two and three glasses at a time by surly waiters in stained aprons. While born of the need for a communal recreation place, it is designed and managed in such a way as to preclude people from enjoying themselves. Liberal and at the same time calvinistic, like the country itself, it forces one to struggle very hard for the least feeling of decadent pleasure or sinful diversion while priding itself on at least having given one that chance. The Yonge Street bars (which themselves would soon close one by one as the musical taste shifted again) were the latest variation. They were dark but too light for comfort, and loud, but with boisterousness, not camaraderie; they were watering holes but not necessarily meeting places. Neither pubs nor American cocktail lounges, they combined the worst features of both and provided music more as background noise than as entertainment.

Like the primitive jazz once thrown up by the New Orleans barrel-houses and gutbuckets, the music that issued from such places needed several characteristics. It needed an amorphous country flavour with none of the ballad aspect of most country music, which required some attention to the narrative. It had to be loud enough to be audible over the general hubbub without triumphing over what little conversation there was. It needed an old-time flavour, to give the customers a sense of partaking in their heritage, yet it couldn't be rustic or primitive enough to let them feel they were being condescended to. The style that emerged in response to such demands was one of great professionalism, slickness, and precision that nonetheless had about it a quality of being somehow homespun. Although the performances were polished, the material reflected semi-rural concerns and an idyllic, countrified past. The Band not only perfected this style, they carried it away and later infused it into the American mainstream.

Robertson and the others, then, were perhaps the first Canadian performers of their generation to make an impact on the course of international pop music without having come out of the folk tradition, though on the surface they were even more continentalist than those who had. Danko has pointed out that although "Levon is from Arkansas, we all got the same stations" on the radio — rock 'n' roll and rhythm–and–blues stations such as WLAC in Nashville. They were squarely in a form of music that was dominated by the United States, not only economically but historically, in Afro-american culture and its white imitations.

After they turned professional, they fell even more within the American sphere of influence. Whichever side of the border they played, they fitted into a scene inspired by the South, both white and Black, whose influence was spread evenly throughout the continent by radio. As Canadians, their experience of the South was transient, of American Blacks, almost nil; they could only recreate, and eventually improve upon, what came to them through the airwaves. In this way they would find themselves in much the same position as the young Dylan except without his folk inheritance. Ralph J. Gleason once wrote that, while earthy, the Band was not funky:

they had the sound down slickly but lacked the soul. Yet coming along when they did, and on the coattails of Dylan who was abandoning folk to help make an art form of rock, they seemed very much part of a new trend. Hawkins has reminisced that the Band was "always two years ahead of their time. Robbie was the first guy to get into white funk, in Canada or anywhere." While he was not adhering to Gleason's fine-line syntax, his point was the same. Being Canadians and, moreover, ones trained in barrooms, they could not help but achieve white earthiness whenever they strove for Black funk. They could not help but seem, in the context of their time, very smooth, very much of a piece, and very American, at least after they began playing with Dylan, whose concern with American mythology no other writer matched for poignancy and breadth.

Their music (mostly tunes by Robertson) was a compound of middle-class technical proficiency and lower-class rough edges, both white and Black. The lyrics (again, usually by Robertson) bear an obvious debt to Dylan in being full of drifters, losers, pistoliers, and gamblers. The total effect is a slick populism that, while distinct, clearly stems from both the rural and the technological worlds. It is partly this fact that caused Greil Marcus, in his book *Mystery Train: Images of America in Rock 'n' Roll Music*, to focus on their imagery and style of playing as immutably, intrinsically, and revealingly American. His chapter on them did much to lift their stature at a time (1975) when they had left Dylan and were flailing about as a group, their best music already behind them, it seemed, struggling to find individual musical identities — a search that led almost inevitably to The Last Waltz. As one critic commented on a song from their final pre-breakup album, ISLANDS, it "might have been written for Greil Marcus of *Rolling Stone*, who can make considerable American Studies hay over this one."

Like everything else about their early years together, the story of how they teamed up with Dylan is masked in contradiction and uncertainty. By one reliable account, Levon and the Hawks were playing in 1963 at the Colonial Tavern on Yonge Street. In the audience was John Hammond, Jr. (whose father was the Columbia A&R man who, in a different era, had signed Benny Goodman and, only two years in the past, Dylan). He was impressed and in 1964 called the Hawks down to New York to work with him on one of his folk albums on the Vanguard label. Contacts made there as studio musicians enabled them to play the local clubs as well, as is still often the case. This plausible story of how they came to play in New York is lent credence by the fact that Robertson later produced one of Hammond's LPs. In any event, it does seem that one evening Mary Martin of

Albert Grossman's office took Dylan to a club in New Jersey to hear them play and that Dylan was equally impressed. He called upon them later when he decided to put together a studio and touring band. The old tales of Dylan himself first having spotted them on Yonge Street are apparently without foundation, as is the one about his telephoning them in Jersey and giving them the job without ever having heard them live. It does appear certain that, when the call came, they were back in Canada and that they did not all leap at the privilege immediately. At first only Robertson, Danko, and Hudson signed on, and Dylan sent his plane for

"Everywhere there was a feeling The Last Waltz was a musical event of intimidating significance."

them. Danko actually left his instruments and amps behind, as Dylan was providing an entirely new set-up. Helm was reluctant to join, perhaps jealous of this takeover of a band he himself had led and, he believed, had held together. For a time Dylan and the Hawks played without him. Even when he did at last capitulate, he at first tried keeping the original group together as a separate act on the side.

By stages, then, they came together as the Band. Although they shot to renown as such, they were being warmed by the reflected glory of Dylan, whose music just then (it was the period between BRINGING IT ALL BACK HOME and HIGHWAY 61 REVISITED) was at its most aggressive, imagistic, and electrically guttural. Robertson's distinctive lead guitar, Danko's swooping bass, Hudson's barrel-house organ, along with Helm's percussion work and the various vocal combinations centred around Manuel, were put to a higher purpose than ever before but also, perforce, relegated to an inferior position on stage. The transition from bars to the electric aesthetic seems a natural one in retrospect, but it would have serious consequences and present a dilemma which they would overcome only by changing directions several times.

Dylan's 1965 tour was the first major swing across the country and abroad since he had ceased being a solo performer in the folk idiom, and the Band was drawn into this important slice of musical history. It took place during the period when (with Robertson present) Dylan is supposed to have been all but booed off the stage by the crowd that had come to Newport expecting a folk concert. He is said to have made the second half of the concert an acoustic set in order to pacify them, but the truth seems to be that he had already decided to begin a transitional period of half-electric, half-acoustic until the mass audience caught up with what were at the time his considerable innovations. One can get some sense of this on a bootleg recording of a concert at the Royal Albert Hall in London in which the Band is brought out to derisive noises that towards the end of the performance magically become cheers — cheers less of delight than of enthused bewilderment at being thrust into a new age.

Throughout their career, the Band were nagged by minor injuries and discommodities, and on that first tour with Dylan, Richard Manuel somehow broke his hand. It now seems as though the injury was almost an omen for what has come to be spoken of as the Accident — a motorcycle crash, in July 1966, near his home in Woodstock, New York, in which Dylan was said to have come close to being killed. For the Band, there must have followed a time of uncertainty about the future: Dylan became a recluse, an object of concern to the outside world and a more introspective writer than at any time in the past. Precisely how long it took him to recover is unclear, but at some point he was back at his music, which was mellower than before.

The Band worked throughout the remainder of the year and through 1967 in seclusion. They were faced with several alternatives. They could look forward in idleness to Dylan's full recovery, awaiting his return to the stage (he was away nine years all told), running the risk that his new music would be too diffuse or personal for their talents. They could pursue individual careers. Or they could continue working with him in Woodstock while also building a group identity for themselves elsewhere. They chose or perhaps merely drifted into the third alternative, but also began to edge in the direction of the second. They sought individual careers *together*; *as a group*, they brought together as a new force what they had learned from Dylan with the best of the Yonge Street school, channelling their common radio heritage through the mixture that Greil Marcus was identifying as the classic American strain in their music, something equivalent in group terms to Joni Mitchell's individualistic ambivalence about America. Alone, Mitchell has always seemed frightened by the place that has continued to pique her curiosity all the same. The Band, as a group entity but one so clearly a group of individuals rather than a single welded whole, found safety. As well as safety in numbers, united with a musical purpose they probably never had as a bar band. They did quite well for themselves.

During 1967 and 1968, they were living in what they called the Big Pink, a house with pink aluminum siding, in West Saugerties, New York. As a group apart from Dylan they had come under the direction of Albert Grossman and remained with him after Dylan himself left the Grossman stable in 1967. So it was that they were preparing songs for their first album under the terms of a contract Grossman had negotiated with Capitol Records. But all the while they were also jamming with their neighbour Dylan, whose new musical direction was still uncertain. The recording was done in the basement of Big Pink on relatively amateurish equipment. It consisted mostly of songs by Robertson and other band members as well as what can only be described as Dylan doodles.

What with his enforced seclusion at the time, Dylan was even more than usual the subject of speculation and rumour, and it was perhaps inevitable that bootlegged, nth-generation tapes and finally a plain-covered album began to circulate. Pressure from the public to release the material officially grew intense. Eventually in 1975 when Dylan was once again touring with the Band and the group's fortunes had undergone several ups and downs, Robertson gathered the originals and edited them into the album entitled BASEMENT TAPES. The release of this LP followed by only a few months that of BEFORE THE FLOOD, a live album of Dylan and the Band together on tour. When compared, the two perhaps illustrate the inevitability of the Band's striking out on their own, as individuals as well as a group, after having been so long typecast, albeit to their profit, as Dylan's backup.

THE BASEMENT TAPES shows first of all the Band's fecundity and versatility as musicians. The majority of the Robertson songs never made it to their first album, and it is a bountiful writer indeed who throws away so many good ideas as he seems to have done. Also, there is a great ambidextrous quality to their musicianship. Danko, the bassist, plays mandolin on one cut, and Hudson, the organist, plays sax, accordion, drums, and harp on others. Robertson plays drums on three different songs, and Helm, who only rejoined his old group after the Dylan material had already been recorded, took up the mandolin. THE BASEMENT TAPES is clearly an instance of homemade music, with necessity vanquishing the problem of resources and helping to lend the whole a spontaneous quality the Band had probably not known since the early days as itinerant honky-tonkers. On all the cuts there is a great deal of cross singing and cross playing. One can almost hear a musical idea initiated by one member being picked up by another, and then by a third, and carried aloft like a volleyball. It is a wonderful example of jazz methodology used for rock ends, a much better example than any found in Joni Mitchell's work, which by comparison seems studied and somewhat mannered.

As far as their relationship with Dylan is concerned, THE BASEMENT TAPES shows that the Band was more than a backup and studio group, however excellent. Instead, the Band joined Dylan in a communalistic, almost utopian enterprise, of which the music as finally released is as much the by-product as the aim. Discography degenerates into meaningless nit-picking as together they become one force working towards some musical purpose not quite clear in their minds. By comparison, BEFORE THE FLOOD is the Band being used purely as auxiliaries. Most of the songs on the four sides are Dylan tunes. "*Knockin' on Heaven's Door*," from his score for Sam Peckinpah's film *Pat Garrett and Billy the Kid*, was the most recent. The album is in large part a retrospective showing of Dylan's material from the previous dozen or so years. That he can keep songs alive in new versions is testament to his skill; unlike Joni Mitchell or Neil Young, he has seldom done studio set pieces and has increasingly come to see his own music as an ongoing stream of activity. But by the very nature of this fact, the Band is put in the background, and one is hard pressed to find a cut on the album in which they seem to be giving their all, and revelling in the joy of doing so, as was often the case on THE BASEMENT TAPES. Even on the one side of BEFORE THE FLOOD made up of Robertson songs, the Band seem somewhat self-conscious or intimidated at sharing the stage with Dylan and the auditorium with those who have come to see him and not themselves.

Listening to these two albums, one gets a sense of what must have been their basic dilemma: how to retain the joy of working together with Dylan without being in his shadow musically or mythologically. They had been playing together for years, developing their particular skills and fitting them together. But except for the euphoria of creating with Dylan, they had received little, by 1968, in the way of reward. The situation was rectified, however, in their first two albums on their own, MUSIC FROM BIG PINK and THE BAND, released in 1968 and 1969 respectively. At least their records, widely acclaimed as some of the brightest rock of the day, helped forestall the inevitable question of how, and in what combinations, and to what purpose they should continue to work together.

As it happened, the music recorded in 1968 and eventually released as THE BASEMENT TAPES bore little relation to what the Band or Dylan himself would eventually get into later that year, one of the most significant in the history of popular music. It was the year, for instance, of Dylan's JOHN WESLEY HARDING, which glowed with a warm inspirational light and helped prove that rock could be used to serious ends previously entrusted to other forms of expression. It was also the year in which Leonard Cohen released his first album, showing that this idea was by no means unattractive to artists traditionally working elsewhere, and of Joni Mitchell's first attempts to reconcile artiness with the art song. In England, the Beatles formed Apple, released YELLOW SUBMARINE and the single "*Lady Madonna*," proving, among other points, that the British invasion was still strong, that junk songs were giving way to thematic works tied to changes in society, and that, in spite of everything, artists failed miserably as capitalists. It was the year of Janis Joplin but also the ascendancy of Los Angeles over San Francisco and the final out-distancing of California as a whole over the Brill Building school of songwriting rooted in New York. The popular song had finally become the dominant art form of the times, and the album, not the single, the medium. An *annus mirabilis* for sure.

But amid the turmoil was a strain of introspection, even melancholy. Musicians pursued individualistic, highly stylized manners in reaction against the furore they themselves were generating; or perhaps they simply found it necessary to elbow out a bit of peace and quiet in which to work. Whatever poignancy many bands seemed to offer became too thin when spread over five or six musicians or else got funnelled into the voice of one member, with the resulting imbalance. In this atmosphere of conflicting personalization and uproar MUSIC FROM BIG PINK at once seemed fresh. Greil Marcus later wrote that in this era only the Band and Grand Funk presented an alternative to what he considered the neutralization of the mainstream by tender, moody loners, such as James Taylor. He saw the Band as a force which, by its simple foot-stomping appeal superimposed on what he took or mistook for their concern with American history, might unify the counterculture forces of the late 1960s now that the Vietnam War was splintering the general population and the various radical factions.

There is some wisdom in that judgement, of course. Here was a band acting like a band. Here, too, was a band with a vitality which seemed to endorse that odd energy in the American character that has always gone hand in hand with violence. And here in MUSIC FROM BIG PINK was evidence of the coming out of a talented songwriting group, though the dominant role played by Robertson in writing the material and leading the group was not fully recognized for he was not prominent vocally. MUSIC FROM BIG PINK was the debut of people who knew what they were doing down to the tiniest detail but whose enthusiasm was unabated, people who knew the kinetic appeal of ragged edges.

The album included "*I Shall Be Released*," a song Dylan had written and himself sang as a prisoner's lament. As performed here, however, it became more of an anguished cry, but one not quite so disturbing as it was joyous in its release of tension. In this way, the song is the verso of "*Tears of Rage*," written by Dylan and Manuel, which is a slow build-up of emotion. The other highlights are the songs written by Robertson, who is clearly under Dylan's influence. Chief among them is "*The Weight*." Like Robertson's most memorable work at this period, the song is musically simple, simplistic even, rather than the work of a self-indulgent or even selfish solo performer. As a result, "*The Weight*" depends on the Band acting communally to put forth its power instrumentally and vocally. The lyric, however, is significant because it shows the heavy hand of Dylan:

I pulled into Nazareth,
was feeling about half past dead
I just need some place to lay my head
Mister, can you tell me
where a man might find a bed?
No, was all he said

Take a load off Fanny
Take a load for free
Take a load off Fanny
and put the load right on me

I picked up my bag,
went looking for a place to hide
then I saw Carman and the Devil
walking side by side
I said, Hey Carman
come on let's go downtown
She said: I gotta go
by my friend can stick around . . .

Here is the implied religiosity of JOHN WESLEY HARDING, which must have been contagious for those working with Dylan in 1967, even though little if any of it surfaced later on THE BASEMENT TAPES. Here, too, is the sudden shift in tenses, the jumping back and forth between legend (in this case, biblical legend) and the sorry realities of the present, so indicative of Dylan. Following through the lyric as a story, it is not clear precisely what the song is saying (Who the hell is Fanny? A modern Mary Magdalene?) or from quite what standpoint. But that itself is the difference between the Band at its best and Dylan at his worst: with them, the experience comes in listening to music being made, not in clinging to the meaning or linear intent of the imagery. One also hears the musical by-play, springing from their barroom days. Various voices keep crossing over one another like Kleig lights, finally meeting in moments of harmony, while Helm's drumming and Danko's bass carry on a mating call.

BIG PINK is at least as important now for its indications of the shift away from Dylan as for its similarities with what he was up to in those days. This is easily shown in the choice to record a song not written by Dylan or a Band member, "*Long Black Veil.*" Written in the manner of a murder ballad, the song tells (from the grave) the story of a man tried and ultimately hanged for murder because his conscience would not allow him to reveal his alibi that on the night in question he was "in the arms of my best friend's wife." The singing is a bit reedy (as is that on "*This Wheel's on Fire*") and lacks the necessary anguish. This problem is an indication that, in common with Dylan and other writers, the Band were unable to put so much energy into other people's songs as into their own. At the same time it also shows that, unlike Dylan, they were perfectly content to induct other people's material into their repertoire when to do so meshed with their own sensibility and image. "Long Black Veil" sounds like a song Robertson could have written, should have written, himself.

This debut album was recorded in two weeks and credits John Simon as producer, though his exact role is open to several interpretations. Their next LP, THE BAND, while made over a longer period of time when they were temporarily free from Dylan, is likewise deliberately homespun. It was recorded in the winter of 1968 at a house they had rented for the purpose in Hollywood. Simon is listed as engineer, though ninety per cent of such work was done by Robertson; Simon's role seems to have been mainly that of sideman, on electric piano, tuba, and an assortment of minor instruments. The album has much less religious flavour than its predecessor but it does have some, the residue of Dylan's influence. Robertson wrote all twelve cuts, though Manuel collaborated on three of them, none distinctive. Robertson's more memorable songs here include "*Across the Great Divide*," "*Rag Mama Rag*," "*Up on Cripple Creek*," and "*The Night They Drove Old Dixie Down*." The last is perhaps his best known song and the one that has helped spur critics in the U.S. to delve into Robertson's Americanism, writing around the fact of his Canadianness as a kind of curious anomaly unworthy of serious consideration.

Virgil Kane is my name
and I served on the Danville train
till Stoneman's cavalry came
and tore up the track again
In the winter of 'sixty-five
we were hungry, just barely alive
I made the run to Richmond itself
It was a time I remember oh so well
The night they drove old Dixie down
and the bells were ringing
The night they drove old Dixie down
and the people were singing . . .

Back with my wife in Tennessee
when one day she called to me
"Virgil quick come see
there goes Robert E. Lee."
Now I don't mind them chopping wood
and I don't care if the money's no good
You take what you need and leave the rest
but they should never have taken the very best

Like my father before me
I'm a working man
and my brother above me
who took a rebel stand.
He was just eighteen, proud and brave

but a Yankee laid him in his grave
I swear by the mud below my feet
you can't raise a Kane back up
when he's in defeat . . .

Obviously an American Civil War song, and one more precisely historical than any by Dylan, whose interest is in blurring past and present, not examining history. While indubitably American in subject, the song is the product of a foreigner trying to learn the historical environment and see

"Anyone who attended a concert by the Band could have sensed the religiosity of their performance."

what it has in common with his own. The reference to Stoneman's federal cavalry tearing up the railway tracks between Danville and Richmond, hardly a matter of textbook history, is clearly the result of research by a curious outsider. Neither does this resemble a Dylan song in reaching into the past for picaresque characters. Robertson is actually trying to get inside the feelings of a single individual a century dead (a fictional character, yes); he finds this necessary in order to transcend nationality, to not emphasize one nationality or the other. This is a song about the human condition, not about the stars and stripes (or the stars and bars of the Confederacy), contrary to the view of many American observers, including Joan Baez who, in her cover of the song, changed two important lines to read:

and I don't care if *my* money's no good

and

here comes *the* Robert E. Lee . . . .

She thus changed the line showing Virgil's altruism in not caring whether he was paid to mean that he was frustrated in being paid in Confederate currency; she also made the glimpse of Lee, the humanitarian general who so hated war and found no peace except in defeat, into a glimpse of a gaudy steamboat.

All of which is to say that in one song Robertson was rejecting everybody else's idea of America. He was going beyond Dylan's America, the land of conmen, carnies, fast women, sloe gin, and everything else that adds to his own mysterious presence as a spokesman for the outcasts. He was also rejecting the textbook America, the radio America. He was coming into his own individual (and hence, because he is a Canadian, Canadian) view of the subject. He was also exerting himself as an individual against the pull of the group, an action bound up both in Canadian society and in religious life. Although he never put it into these terms, Robertson was rejecting the contrived and unsubtle spirituality of Dylan, or Cohen for that matter, and coming instead to confront some basic spiritual questions.

Anyone who attended a concert by the Band could have sensed the religiosity of their performance without quite being conscious of it. This is especially true of their later concerts, when they had far exceeded the life expectancy of most groups and already lived out in public many highs and lows. Such extremes were occasioned by, or at least somehow linked to, the sacrifice of individual talents to the glory of the group. For many years, and until Robertson really blossomed as a songwriter, no one member had stood out in the public's mind as the best or even best known. The subordination of the individual to the whole probably accounted in large part for the tightness of their music. But the threat of one or more of them being detrimental to the group also gave the Band the jagged edges that made their sound so uncommon. The resulting tension between these jagged edges and the slick core of their sound always lent the Band an angularity obvious to the public who never read the trade press or heard the stories about their doings. The tautness running through their music and their group career doubtless has political correlatives. Yet the religious overtones were always somehow more blatant than the political ones, especially in their live performances once they had completed the 1966 Dylan tour.

This tension between individual fulfilment and group or community solidarity runs through most religions, in which both views have their place. In Christianity, the individual who strives for his own purification and union with God can be either truly alone and private, like St. Anthony, or can make a display of his solitude; either way, the individual gets out of the body and is subject to ecstatic visions and demonic bad trips. One felt traces of such attitudes in the concerts, in which the Band seemed to struggle together but nevertheless as individuals, with fits of despair and moments of near ecstasy in their music, seldom acknowledging the audience but, by the simple fact of their being on stage, allowing the audience to take part.

The liturgical substitute for the holy solitary hero is the ritual mass, and here again the Band's quasi-religious posture is evident, in the elaborate ritual of course, but also in the way the participants dissolve anonymously into their roles. In style if not in importance and solemnity, comparison with the Last Waltz is obvious. Just as the brightly lit, expensively mounted cathedral show is both a foretaste of heaven and a stylized retelling of the central story, so the Waltz was both an exposition on the group's breakup and a foretelling of their reincarnation, as individual performers at one with their particular muses, exemplars of personal heroism. But the metaphor need by no means be Christian, for all salvation-after-death religions have such individual peace at the end, and in many systems the oneness or the community of the blessed is anticipated on earth by ritual society (though of course, some don't allow for any such end: in Buddhism, the state of nirvana eliminates the individual altogether). In any case, there was something Christian about the Band that went beyond the debt to

Anglican hymns especially obvious on the LP, THE BAND.

Robertson, Danko, Manuel, and Hudson were all born in Methodist Ontario and behaved like Methodists in their careers in that while part of a viable unit, they also carried on behind the scenes as individuals, to some profit. Characteristic of individual Ontario Methodists is the tendency to suddenly become Anglicans once they have made their fortunes. One can see the same process at work here. During the Canadian years and when playing with Hawkins on both sides of the border, the musicians were musical Methodists, polishing individual skills for future use but content for the time being with applying them to the betterment of the group. But then, after touring with Dylan, when after his mishap they became star attractions in their own right, they could no longer continue in subservience, and so become musical Anglicans — content only with a higher sort of theatre, of which the Last Waltz is the best example. In any event, the process can easily be traced through the music they recorded, and the individual courses they pursued, in the decade between the two sets of Dylan tours.

No one would say that the Band is rooted in folk music the way Gordon Lightfoot, Leonard Cohen, and Joni Mitchell are. Yet it is hard to deny that they were rooted in the atmosphere of folk as it has always existed in Canada. This was most obvious in the homespun flavour of their music and especially the way they packaged it. There is something intrinsically Canadian, for example, in the spectacle of one of the most sophisticated studio bands ever assembled continuing to record their albums under semi-professional conditions in basements, rented houses, and small theatres. This bespeaks an uneasiness with urbanity and a need to return to simpler times, the electronic counterpart of one's frontier heritage.

Such folky independence is also shown in other ways — the way in which they for so long eschewed even colour photographs of themselves on their jackets or the way in which they toured and went on television only when they felt like doing so. This shows independence, but not the insouciant Anglican kind of someone who has made his bundle and now does what he or she damn well pleases. Rather, it is the independence of one who, like some 1960s folksinger, wants to preserve the spontaneity and closeness of live performances.

Thus the Band, in the long years between the two periods of touring with Dylan, appeared in concert when they required live applause or had fresh material to give, not merely when they had a new album to sell. Similarly, they did television only when they could work live, thus preserving at least some of the energy and kick of working with an audience. For this reason they once appeared on *Saturday Night Live*— indeed, had once done the *Ed Sullivan Show* (in 1970, the same year they made the cover of *Time*). Those were signs that their popular reputation was firmly established as a band apart. But such publicity also showed they were going in a direction that, deep down, none of them perhaps sought. They were in danger of drifting together towards glittery success when clearly what their consciences dictated was drifting separately to individual fulfilment. Apparently, they came to realize this danger slowly, judging from the albums they produced during the years in question.

After MUSIC FROM BIG PINK and THE BAND, when they were no longer thoroughly associated with Dylan except in memory, some critics were at a loss to explain what seemed their sudden excellence. Yet neither could they continue as though their own work were a sideline. They were *the* Band and they had to do something to evolve from past associations, if not actually repudiate them. What they produced were four albums in as many years which taken together now show the way they sometimes grasped at straws as the Band, but in some cases grew and developed as individuals. The albums are STAGE FRIGHT (1970), CAHOOTS (1971), ROCK OF AGES (1972), and MOONDOG MATINEE (1973).

Recorded as it was in so short a time and partly for the apparent fun of it, BIG PINK had been a casual album. By contrast, THE BAND was well considered and carefully, though conservatively, produced. It was a conceptual album; right down to the jacket, it bore the message of the way human individuality becomes lost in the maddeningly consistent flow of history, till only humanity remains. The vitality of the album came from the interaction of five musicians, not from such mechanical processes as mixing and overdubbing, of which it had none. The result was a rendering of great diversity, power, and immediacy with a consistent tone. STAGE FRIGHT (Robertson is said to have taken the name of the title song from the 1950 Hitchcock film) is the opposite. It is in no way a conceptual album, being made up of songs of many different musical types, including some that bore the stamp of THE BAND and several others ("*The W.S. Walcott Medicine Show*," for example) which were well regarded individually. Despite this, the songs achieve what in those circumstances is the well nigh impossible feat of all sounding alike.

Partly this is because, as the title song indicates, the responsibility of being a single act in the big time weighed heavily on them. Their vitality was beginning to wane. STAGE FRIGHT, recorded at the Woodstock Playhouse, showed some of their musical differences. The LP coincided with suggestions that the Band was in financial trouble; the rumours were exaggerated if not false, and one must be careful not to fall into the trap which so many Canadian journalists have fallen into with Hawkins, of making the highs seem higher and the lows lower than they actually were. Still, it was not a good time for them professionally or musically, at least as a group entity. Albert Grossman would shortly leave the management business to run the Bearsville label. From that point on, handling of the group was more casual, and much of the burden appears to have fallen on Robertson, who by that time was of course already the mainstay creatively. He would assume the latter position even more noticeably on the next album, with even poorer musical results for the future of the group.

In CAHOOTS one sees the Band at a loss for what to do following the decided lack of success of STAGE FRIGHT. Whether or not by design, the album they released tried to marry what they hoped would gain them renewed attention and respect. Representing the former Band sound was a country tune apparently from Dylan's NASHVILLE SKYLINE period of several years earlier. The other songs were all Robertson's. Though one of these, "*4% Pantomime*," was written and previously recorded by Van Morrison, whose presence may only have further driven apart the Band, most were written under the Dylan influence lyrically. And "*Last of the Blacksmiths*" can be interpreted as one of Robertson's slips into Canadianism:

> Who robbed the cradle? Who robbed the grave?
> Who's the one that asked to be saved?
> No, no answer.
>
> I moved to a country that cried of shame
> I left my home and found a name
> No, nobody could explain.
>
> Have mercy cried the blacksmith,
> how you gonna replace human hands?
> Found guilty said the judge
> for not being in demand.
>
> Frozen fingers at the keyboard
> could be his reward . . .
> Dead tongues said the poet
> to the daughter of burlesque
> Cocteau, Van Gogh and Geronimo
> they used up what was left.

This seems almost a parody of Dylan's diction and vocabulary, especially the lines about the judge and condemned man as well as the line tossing out the names of unrelated artists and Indians. But it also goes beyond parody in a way characteristic of the Canadian songwriters in the U.S. The references to the freeze-up at the piano and the fear of slipping into commercial and artistic disrepute are almost touching; if the song were a dream, Freudians would rejoice at the discovery of the author's attempts to mask his neurotic creativity in the closeness of the group. Such an outburst of frankness from Robertson came amid some newfound frailty on the part of the others, as though on cue they had forgotten almost everything they had learned about being a band.

On "*Masterpiece,*" for instance, they try desperately to emit a hillbilly sound rather than the rockabilly one they became so adept at under Hawkins. They fail to be convincing because they cannot help being polished. The same holds true for "*Shoot Out in Chinatown,*" another of Robertson's historical songs; although one of the album's high spots, it shows the Band being simply too smooth for their own good. At this time they had lost or put aside most of the roughness which had made them so distinctive. There are few if any solos, and so hardly any of the game of musical hot-potato at which they excelled. The whole album is further marred by curious production. Unwilling to revert to the simplicity of their first two albums but all too eager to experiment alone on behalf of the group, Robertson goes wild. Allen Toussaint, the New Orleans producer, was brought in to arrange a horn section, which pops up jarringly throughout; and in the mixing stage, the treble was accentuated while the bass was forced way down. The result is a disjointed musical hodgepodge, even though Robertson was emerging from this muddle of his own making as a forceful and poignant stylist.

Robertson's strengths would only be displayed fully on the next album, which was another complete turnabout. ROCK OF AGES, the Band's only live album without Dylan, was culled from a three-night engagement at the New York Academy of Music spanning New Year's Day, 1972. It is in many ways a remarkably fine album, incorporating the correction of old errors (here Toussaint's horns seem in place) and presentation of new strengths (a remarkable array of jazz men skilfully used). The material was for the most part old. Arguably, this is the "best" of the Band, not the later album so titled. Here the members reassert themselves and much of the old magic is evident. If musically it is their most cohesive effort, in other ways it is simply procrastination. They come together once more as the Band, that remarkable creature with ten hands, five voices, and a life of its own, and do all that they were ever praised for doing. But the album confirms their basic problem without solving it. It makes plain all their conflicts — Canadian versus American, the group versus the individual, and so on.

With the next LP they reverted to an earlier stage. MOONDOG MATINEE (the title is that of a radio program Hudson remembered listening to as an adolescent in Canada) is a 1950s nostalgia album. It was as though the Band, for all its links to radio and its roadhouse rockabilly training, were somehow unconnected with that decade except in the most mechanical and contrived ways. In truth, they had always been far older in spirit, at times almost ancient, and centrally wrapped up in expressing the problem of how to reconcile such feelings with the medium of rock. Most of the feeling, of course, emanated from the lyrics, and these overwhelmingly had been the work of Robertson, an artist who, for all his affection for the American experience, has many traits common in certain Canadian careers.

There was an old joke in those days about a struggling young Canadian actor who goes to Hollywood seeking work. He is interviewed by an agent who distractedly asks him about his previous credits, not expecting much in the way of a reply. The actor, not sensing the older man's mood, explains matter of factly that he had been given his own ill-fated series on the CBC, done experimental theatre in Toronto garages, worked in four domestic feature films whose budgets ran into three figures, made do between times with cabaret upstairs above Italian restaurants — and oh yes, he's also done Shakespeare, musical comedy, road-company rock opera in the nude, and still receives small residual cheques from three commercials. The agent, in a way uncharacteristic of agents, falls from his chair in amazement. The kid, though broke, has certainly been around.

The anecdote is funny if at all only because it is so frequently true. The nature of Canadian culture forces artists and artisans to try their hand at a number of activities in order to make a living, with the result that generalists are more common and are considered less remarkable than in many other countries whose cultures tend towards specialization. Dramatic actors are also nightclub comics, publishers serve as social critics, poets work as editors and publicists, and no one finds the situation particularly unusual. It is stretching a point to state that Robertson fits into this Canadian context, but it is no exaggeration to say that he at least fits the pattern of such people.

"I would say that when I was fourteen there was no turning back," he has said in an interview. "By then I was pretty sure that I wanted to be a professional musician." For him being a professional musician does not stop at playing his chosen instrument. He considers it first necessary to devise the music he will later play. In this he is slightly different from the songwriter who is also a singer and from the performer who also composes; for him the two processes are one. Considered strictly as a musician,

*"Robertson is one of
those infuriatingly
gifted people who
seems to move with ease
from one instrument
to another."*

Robertson is one of those infuriatingly gifted people who seems to move with ease from one instrument to the next and even from one family of instruments to another, never losing sight of what he wants the instruments and himself to create together. Similarly, he is also a skilled arranger, a shrewd manager, an inventive promoter, an ingenious producer of records — his own and other musicians' — and a keen spotter of newcomers. Having himself as much talent as is found in many another entire group, he was doubly useful to his own band. But perhaps he was also doubly frustrated by the group's inability to satisfy all his ambitions.

Robertson cannot of course be singled out as the only member of the Band with a broad base and a sharp appreciation of the times. Each member is somehow extraordinary in his own way. Danko, whose father was a classical musician who also played country, had no formal training either, and simply developed his bass style from listening to such people as Edgar Willis (who played with Ray Charles) and Ron Carter and from listening to Motown. He probably was the first musician to use the transistor bass amp. Hudson, also an early disciple of Detroit where he played for a time before joining the Hawks, helped Yamaha develop a new polyphonic synthesizer. Between gigs, he used to teach the other members music theory. Helm actually spent the summer of 1972 improving his knowledge at the Berklee College of Music in Boston; significantly, he afterward seemed to become increasingly individualistic and so to militate somewhat against the group's shared originality. But most of the suasion, like the majority of the talent, stemmed from Robertson. Always the group's principal songwriter, especially after the first two albums, he simply became so good a one that he shone more brightly than they did, despite his usual modesty and shyness of the limelight. Stating that the main influence on his writing was Dylan is as accurate as it is obviously true. He came to share many of Dylan's concerns. But he quickly bent them to his own design and distinctive style, much as Dylan himself had done with the music of Guthrie and other old folksingers and blues men.

Robertson was first of all a guitarist and that fact accounted for his earliest associations with Dylan. His lead work is some of the most solid available. With his incredibly fast picking technique and other traits of style (some of which he has said he developed from trying to imitate Muddy Waters without using a slide), he has made his sound easily identifiable. It was mainly in such a capacity that he played backup on Dylan's BLONDE ON BLONDE, which was released in 1966, a few months before the Accident, once Dylan and the Band had already been touring together and had recorded one single, *"Can You Please Crawl Out Your*

Window." Apparently, Robertson began writing in volume only after the motorcycle spill, but even then he was working closely with Dylan. Like Manuel, he is credited as co-author on a couple of Dylan songs, having written the melodies. So it is natural that Robertson would have leaned towards Dylan's style and outlook, but in view of his outsider position, similar in a way to Joni Mitchell's, it is also logical that he should have at the same time contrasted sharply with such a style.

Obviously Dylan and Robertson come out of the same general roots in music, though just as obviously they take somewhat different shape when each works without the other. What in Dylan is black syncopated despair comes out in the Band sounding like African highlife music, and in Robertson's work itself as a less joyous, more introspective kind of blues. For all that, Dylan left in Robertson traces of the tradition foreign to the radio-weaned Canadian honky-tonker. The song *"Up on Cripple Creek"* on the Band's second album, for instance, is inspired by the old fiddle tune *"Cripple Creek."* Robertson undoubtedly heard the original from Dylan or was led by him into searching out such songs. The largely unrecorded Ontario fiddle tradition is as noticeably lacking in Robertson as it is in Gordon Lightfoot.

The greater inheritance from Dylan was a certain sense of unofficial history and an understanding of how it could be applied to songwriting. And historical songs were long Robertson's forte. On the first two Band albums this historical sense infected the other players and imparted a unity to the finished records; in later releases, it kept recurring boldly. Such was the case on NORTHERN LIGHT/SOUTHERN CROSS, their 1975 album, which was recognized as perhaps the most substantial record since the bootlegs of the basement tapes, whose ultimate official release it followed by a few months. This LP features all the characteristic elements. The general tone is one of mellowness combined with raucousness. There is also the telltale dexterity of the individual members. *"Ophelia,"* for example, a sort of demented love song by Robertson, is a simple and tuneful piece whipped up into something special with dixieland vamping and a crazy organ. Yet the most telling aspect of the record is Robertson's ongoing effort to write himself through and beyond the Dylan style.

At his most characteristic, Dylan is two kinds of writer. There is Dylan the imagist, who rolls out strings of flashy and often memorable metaphors and individual lines, sometimes for serious ends, at other times for comedic or satiric purposes. Then there is Dylan the storyteller, writing ballads and relating snatches of plausibly ancient stories. Robertson worked in both these motifs. There is one song on the album, *"Ring Your Bell,"* which is a fine instance of the two by turns.

Ring your bell
change your number
run like hell
you can't hide from thunder
Oh no

Ring your bell
get in the wind
You and me gonna
make some medicine

Run that rebel across the tracks
with the mountains on this trail
He was taught "Don't get caught
at the mercy of the man,
land in jail . . ."

**SOME
DAY
SOON**

The first two stanzas are pure nonsense; at least, they circumvent the concrete statement. But the sudden divebombing of imagery leaves one with strong intimations of carnality on the lam. Indeed, as done by the Band, the song sounds incredibly sexy. The third stanza, however, begins to resemble one of Dylan's imitation murder ballads as it slips from the bawdiness of the present into a view of the past filled not with unsung anti-heroes (as in Dylan's work) but with ordinary people who represent their time while in no way shaping it.

The best example of this kind of transition on the album is "*Acadian Driftwood*," which is also Robertson's clearest statement on the condition of being a Canadian in the United States:

The war was over
and the spirit was broken
The hills were smoking
as the men withdrew

We stood on the cliffs
and watched the ships
slowly sinking
to their rendezvous

They signed a treaty
and our homes were taken,
loved ones forsaken
They didn't give a damn

Try to raise a family
end up the enemy
of what went down
on the Plains of Abraham

Acadian driftwood
gypsy tailwinds
They call my home
the land of snow

"Canadian cold front
moving in"
What a way to ride
Oh what a way to go . . .

This isn't my turf
This ain't my season
Can't think of one reason
to remain . . .

Set my compass north
Got winter in my blood

Clearly this is a song about the expulsion of Acadians, told from the point of view of one of their descendants, whom Robertson has no trouble imagining himself to be. But it is not a historical song like those that came from Johnny Horton in the late 1950s and early 1960s, for it takes a humane and sophisticated view of history and sees the past in terms of persons not much different from ourselves in their problems and aspirations — not the flag-and-bugle history of Hollywood movies. While acutely aware of the differences between then and now, "*Acadian Driftwood*" plays up the similarities between us and our forebears, evoking our sympathy. Robertson obviously needs little provocation to think this way; his sentiments are with his subject. He feels kinship with those exiled from us by death now that he himself is exiled, as it were, in the United States.

Perhaps his choice of Canadian subject is a natural outcome of the situation. Like Joni Mitchell, Robertson turns to Canadian subjects for consolation the way one buys one's hometown paper at those stands in Times Square and Hollywood Boulevard, just to see if the old place remains standing, to show that one still cares. But because he is more a journalist and less an autobiographer than Mitchell, he does not turn to his own childhood, as she does. Although, like her, he reaches for the stock images of Canada ("winter in my blood"), he also quickly refutes them — as in the line about TV weather reports, the main source of Canadian references for most Americans. This song is written from the outsider's position; it tries (as the Quebec government has tried) to link Acadians of Louisiana with the landscape their ancestors left two centuries ago. This attempt may be traced in some measure to the letting down of internal, sectarian borders that seems to naturally accompany home thoughts from abroad. It may also be significant that his wife, Dominique, is a *Canadienne* from Montreal and so herself probably aware of the meaning of double exile.

For all that, the key line of the song must be the one about being "the enemy of what went down on the Plains of Abraham." The enemies (that is, victims) of history are common in Robertson's songs, even in less serious ones. He illustrates that the little people who get trampled by events, not the politicos, warriors, and nabobs, are the substance of history. In this way Virgil Kane, an American, and the unnamed Acadian, at least a putative Canadian, are alike. This is a higher level of historical thought than one finds in Dylan, whose deepest understanding of people unlike himself comes in such early songs as "*Restless Farewell*," about an iron ore miner's widow in the present day, though like Dylan, Robertson is a fervent believer in using modern music to bring history to the public.

Robertson has captured the diction of an earlier time and of a type of person now extinct or nearly so. But he does not ruin this mastery of the semi-literate's simple eloquence by making what he writes into imitation folk songs. Some people were annoyed by the use of the idiom "what went down," claiming that it ruined for them the song's historical sense. But Robertson is only doing what artists have always done in dealing with history by putting it into the only contemporary context he knows, which itself will one day add to the song's historical appeal. In *Aristotle Contemplating the Bust of Homer*, Aristotle is depicted in the garb of a seventeenth-century Flemish burgher, not that of an ancient Greek. Does that make Rembrandt's painting "inaccurate" or in any way interfere with what he wanted to express? The means of expression merely helps place the artist in as clear a context as his subject.

Robert Christgau has stated that only Robertson and Dylan have managed to write worthwhile dramatic songs in this fictive form, but that is not quite accurate. Many of the most talented contemporary songwriters of the generation under review have done so on occasion, often with fine results. One thinks of Paul Simon's "*Duncan*" (about a Maritimer's sexual awakening in New England) and "*The Boxer*" or even Loudon Wainwright's "*Prince Hal's Dirge*," a marvellous marriage of medium hard rock and Shakespeare's *Henry IV*. It is simply that Robertson mastered the deeply felt historical song and worked in the form for quite a few years, so that he practically made it his own. The early songs, such as "*The Night They Drove Old Dixie Down,*" may have shown others the possibilities of this approach. What does seem certain is that his development as a remarkable songwriter made him far and away the most immediately recognizable of an exceptional group of musicians, thus rendering the cordial split of the Band all the more unavoidable.

After NORTHERN LIGHTS/SOUTHERN CROSS, which had been recorded, typically, at what they called Shangri-la, a jerry-rigged studio they built for themselves in a house on the Pacific Coast Highway in Malibu, they still had one album to go on their Capitol contract. By that time, they had reached the decision to cease performing together, even though they might well record together later. The Last Waltz was being planned; the recording and filming of it had already been arranged. Apparently it was with the intention of withholding the live album (probably for some other label) that, with one week to go, they made their final pre-breakup album, ISLANDS. Naturally enough in the circumstances, it lacks the cohesiveness, the single voice, of some of the earlier work, though it has many significant moments. "*Knockin' Lost John,*" for example, is another of Robertson's historical songs, this time about the Depression. Again, a brass section is used to better effect than it was originally on CAHOOTS. On the whole, ISLANDS is an album of the telling phrase and the well-timed riff but, just as fittingly, one of departures as well. The title song, for instance, is an instrumental; and two other cuts are from outsider sources. Robertson said he included Hoagy Carmichael's "*Georgia on My Mind*" as his part in helping the presidential campaign of Jimmy Carter. Done in a country version, this song has probably never been delivered with more feeling and panache. By its inclusion, then, the song was a political statement, and so perhaps another sign that the Band's "lyricist, manager, strategist, savant, visionary and spokesman" had become more than that. However involuntarily and inevitably, the Band had become his band, even more completely than it had been Hawkins' or Dylan's. Such a situation was clearly untenable for people of such sensitivity and enterprise.

Long before the Last Waltz, Robertson in various ways became more prominent outside the Band. In 1970 he had "discovered" Jesse Winchester, the Tennessee draft exile in Canada whose sensuous homespun music so resembles the Band's early records. He produced Winchester's first album. By 1976 he produced Neil Diamond's BEAUTIFUL NOISE, becoming the first producer to receive billing on the sleeve equal to the performer's.

The Last Waltz was of course the official signal that the Band could not bear this tension any longer — and that a certain period in rock history had ended. The documentary film Martin Scorsese made of the event was an historical film most of all. But it was also a reconfirmation of whence the Band (or four of them) had come. The breakup was not really a breakup, just a withdrawal of services as concert artists. Even on their funeral they collaborated to make the ceremony unusual, memorable, and friendly. The end came neither with a bang nor a whimper but a waltz, which is neither celebratory nor elegiac but only, somehow, warmly official and proper. The termination of the Band as it had been known for so long was not a divorce or a going of separate ways so much as a coldly-arrived-at realization that the inevitable had finally overtaken them.

The most incisive criticism of the Last Waltz, or rather of Scorsese's *Last Waltz*, came from a source not ordinarily thought of in connection with popular music. Writing in *Saturday Night*, Robert Fulford laid out the rationale for the breakup, as Robertson explained it in the film with such eloquence: after sixteen years as a bar band and then a star band, they had had enough of the road. Fulford disagreed:

> This premise is nonsense. The Band members long ago reached that level of success at which they could shape their careers without any reference to the demands of 'the road'. They could settle in Dallas or Timbuktu, play a concert down the street whenever they felt like it, make records, and survive prosperously. They, not the exigencies of the business, have determined the course of their working lives, at least since the early 1970s. No, the reason for the concert in San Francisco was quite different. It was an attempt to push The Band into that theatrical supra-musical world in which so much of pop music has existed now for years — the same world which gives us, in quite a different mood, staged phenomena like Alice Cooper and Kiss. The Band wanted to organize its own mythology, in the style of 1970s rock, and the San Francisco concert (and this film which is the record of it and a major reason for it) was a way to create a drama. In this sense the occasion was an enormous success as a shrewdly and meticulously prepared presentation of a corporate image.

Yet however contrived the image might have been, the event being observed was designed not to propagate it but rather to enshrine or entomb it. Members of the Band played together in different combinations thereafter (and by 1970 Danko was hinting in the press of a possible reunion album), but as individuals they moved on to other concerns. So charismatic was Robertson on the screen that many prophesied an immediate career for him in movies, though his acting began and ended with an unimportant film called *Carny*. His real film work came in the form of writing scores for Scorsese projects such as *Raging Bull*, *The King of Comedy*, and *The Colour of Money*. It was Levon Helm who made a name for himself as a Hollywood actor. Danko, who shared only four writing credits on the Band's ten albums (though one of them was "*Wheels on Fire*") had been the first one to break away, setting up a parallel career as a solo artist a year before the Waltz. He put together a new group for himself and thrived.

"So charismatic was Robertson on the screen that many prophesied an immediate career for him in the movies."

Garth Hudson, too, remained active as a musician solely, but less conspicuously so than Danko, but then he always had been the reclusive member of the gang. Richard Manuel committed suicide in a Florida motel room in 1986; he hanged himself (just as Roy Buchanan would do in 1988).

And what of Robertson, from whom so much was not merely expected but presumed? The solo album to which his mind must have returned again and again during the Last Waltz days, and about which he certainly began to give interviews as early as 1978, did not appear until 1987. ROBBIE ROBERTSON, produced by Daniel Lanois, the expatriate Canadian who also did Dylan's OH MERCY, had a theme of sorts: Robertson, whose mother was a Mohawk, claimed to have discovered his Native heritage, and peppered the album with Indian imagery, but much of it sounded like the Hollywood Indian type (one song was called "*Broken Arrow*" for God's sake). His writing was strong but jagged, with one memorable melody as such, "*Somewhere Down the Crazy River*," which provided the basis of a video, again with a Native motif. Garth Hudson played keyboards on two cuts, Danko sang background vocals on another, but there was no trace of the Band's personality, none of the old-timey flavour or the big-dog friendliness. He had gone far beyond all that. But where? He drew on such a diverse bunch of guest artists, from U2 to BoDeans, that it almost seemed as though their presence was intended to support him. More that one reviewer noticed that he appears to adopt the style of whomever he was playing with on a particular track. The songs were far more musically complex than what he had done in the Band but lacked strength because . . . Because in the last analysis Robertson turned out, irony of ironies, to be a group artist after all, one who was lost without the communal experience.

five

NEIL YOUNG
"That's My Sound, Man"

*"Neil Young
sounds like the
wind on the
Prairies."*

When a dozen post-punkers put their talents together in 1989 to create THE BRIDGE: A TRIBUTE TO NEIL YOUNG, it was a small but significant statement on Young's influence as a primitive, and it raised a question that had to be addressed. Although he is far too important a musician and songwriter to be categorized as a transitional figure, Neil Young does represent the end of the evolutionary process these essays have tried to illustrate and also therefore the beginnings of the rather different musical climate that took form in the 1980s. He too came out of the folk revival, an acoustic performer who stood up in coffee houses armed with a guitar, but more than any of the others he has been drawn to new styles and new media. His experiments with elaborate stage shows, then film, and finally video may not always have been successful, but they have always been sincere; he has been honestly intrigued by new possibilities, not, like so many others of his generation, simply conscious of the need to go where market forces beckon. It is not simply by happenstance that he has been the only person written about in these pages who has tried to take to video as a new musical medium, rather than simply treat it the way Joni Mitchell or Robbie Robertson have done — which is the way Charlie Chaplin treated motion pictures with sound. This willingness may in turn be tied to his success in shedding so much of the lone performer's ego that always seemed to go with the folk aesthetic.

In a memoir entitled *Neil and Me*, Scott Young lists the various bands, both professional and amateur, with which his son was associated in Winnipeg. Their very names — Stardust, the Jades, the Esquires, the Squires — conjure up the era perfectly, post-hipster but pre-hippie. When he relocated in Toronto in 1965, at the height of the Yorkville folk culture, Young was part of the Mynah Birds, which had the backing of John Craig Eaton of the department-store family and could claim to be the first white group to record for the Motown label (a distinction roughly equivalent to appearing in the first modern-dress production of *The Count of Monte Cristo*). The elder Young goes on to recount how his son and a friend then "sold everything they had and (in Neil's phrase) 'some things we didn't have' " and moved on to Los Angeles, driving an old Pontiac hearse. Once there he joined Buffalo Springfield, formed Crazy Horse, entered the firm of Crosby, Stills & Nash, put together groups called the Stray Gators and the Santa Monica Flyers, revived Crazy Horse, recorded and toured with Trans Band, founded the Shocking Pinks (later reinventing them as the Redwood Boys), and then created the International Harvesters, before reuniting with CSN&Y after an absence of more than a decade, without ever really ceasing to be, except for a few years, a solo performer primarily.

Quite an accomplishment, and in some elusive but immutable way, quite Canadian, too.

Looking at Neil Young is a different activity from looking at Lightfoot, Cohen, Mitchell, Robertson, or almost any other similar figure, because of the existence of his father's book. It has nothing of the fan-gazing that characterizes most writing about such people. Nor, amazingly, does it seem to lose more insights than it gains into the subject or his work by reason of their relationship. Scott Young is a long-time journalist and writer of fiction who brought a lot of craft knowledge to the job of reporting on his son while, at the same time, giving readers the benefit of his emotional proximity to the personalities and events he describes. Unfortunately, the quality of this no doubt unique document has been overlooked, though solely on the basis of its usefulness as a biographical source it is certainly too conspicuous to ignore.

The bare facts are that Neil Young was born in Toronto in 1945 when his father was an assistant editor at *Maclean's*. By a margin of two years, he was the younger of a pair of sons (the other one, Robert, would grow up to serve time in prison in the 1980s and 1990s for drug trafficking). According to his father, who doesn't seem much given to romantic revisionism, Neil Young showed musicality even as an infant but was otherwise "normal." He had the type of customary traumas children survive (nearly drowned at three, polio scare at five). But the greater event awaited him in adolescence, shortly after he began teaching himself the guitar by using a ukulele, when his parents separated and he moved to Manitoba with his mother. Guilt flowed. The senior Young remarks that even "years later I used to see myself in every miserable bastard who showed up in Neil's songs" (though not as the old man in "Old Man / take a look at my life / I'm a lot like you" which is about someone else entirely, according to its author).

At eighteen Young was doing his best to break into the music business. His father quotes a letter from the boy's mother informing him that "Neil has decided to follow your advice and become a dropout." A Toronto agent told him he wasn't experienced enough to work solo and didn't yet have the knack of assembling the right people to play with. So he picked up whatever work he could around Yorkville and farther afield. It was while playing in the Lakehead, for example, that he first met Stephen Stills, who at this time could have been described as a New York folkie. Later, when he lit out for California, it was partly with the intention of looking up Stills, and they both became part of Buffalo Springfield.

The Canadian music scene was quite small and people in it tended to share complicated personal histories. When Young was in high school,

*"Young was an
irrepressible team
player yet a restless
individualist."*

he would cut classes to go listen to a local guitar virtuoso. Another Winnipeg kid, from a different high school, would do the same. The virtuoso was Lenny Breu; the other kid was Randy Bachman, later of the Guess Who and Bachman-Turner Overdrive, whose father was a local country singer. Similarly, Young had known Joni Mitchell for years through her husband Chuck Mitchell, who had played around Winnipeg at about that same time. Now he found that such overlapping acquaintanceships were no less a feature of the Los Angeles scene. For example, the keyboardist Jack Nitzsche, who was important in Mitchell's work, would also figure in Young's career (and later in his personal life as well, for in 1979 Nitzsche was acquitted of raping Young's former mate, the actress Carrie Snodgress).

There was a strange egalitarianism in Los Angeles that seems surprising in a city that worships success even more than it worships the sun. On one memorable occasion after he had begun recording, but long before his career was assured, Young found himself jamming with John Lennon, George Harrison, and Ringo Starr. Members of the local fraternity always seemed to be combining and recombining in search of the perfect mix of talents, a goal which, if and when achieved, might prove so fleeting as to seem unreal. In such a bubbling atmosphere Young bobbed to the surface in 1967 when Buffalo Springfield (the name was taken from a make of earth-moving equipment) brought out its first album, also called BUFFALO SPRINGFIELD, which included the single "*For What It's Worth (Stop, Hey What's That Sound)*." With its repetitious suggestion of drug-induced disorientation and its musical allusion to the so-called San Francisco sound (it would have fitted comfortably on Jefferson Airplane's SURREALISTIC PILLOW), "*For What It's Worth*" became a signature tune of the late 1960s; among people of a certain age, hearing it again even for a moment brings back memories of where they at least *hoped* they were and what they *thought* they were doing when it was first getting airplay. To know that Young left the group in an argument over whether or not appearing on Johnny Carson's television show was, *ipso facto*, a counter-revolutionary act (with Young taking the affirmative) is to know much about the timbre of the times.

Such partings, however, were not necessarily permanent, as his later career would show, though reunions were often postponed because rapid-fire developments kept intervening, as happened in this case. Within a year, Jim Messina and Richie Furay of the Springfield had formed another band, Poco. Young had taken up with a group called the Rockets who later became the redoubtable Crazy Horse. He had married for the first time. And he had launched a solo career on Warner with his album NEIL

YOUNG, on which Dr. John and Ry Cooder performed. That was 1968. Within one twelve-month period, he would release that album and a second one, EVERYBODY KNOWS THIS IS NOWHERE, and the third and final Springfield album, LAST TIME AROUND.

The comings and goings grow more complex, circumstantial, and illusory. Virtually simultaneous with EVERYBODY KNOWS THIS IS NOWHERE came the first album by Crosby, Stills & Nash — David Crosby, who a couple of years earlier had been expelled from the folk-rock group the Byrds, whose opening act Buffalo Springfield had once been; Stills, now at loose ends following Springfield's break-up; and Graham Nash, late of the Hollies. The sense of a small pool of talent runs counter to the speed with which events were moving. Young didn't abandon Crazy Horse nor his solo identity (AFTER THE GOLD RUSH followed in 1970 after no more than a decent interval) in order to pursue Crosby, Stills & Nash. In the minds of many people, the group will always be associated with their version of Joni Mitchell's song "*Woodstock*" on the soundtrack of the film of the same name. On the sound track only, for Mitchell wrote the song after the event, in somewhat the same way Young would write "*Ohio*" for the DÉJÀ VU album within days of the shootings at Kent State: telltale signs, in both cases, of careers begun in folk coffee houses.

The fact that Young chose to lead a double life in his career seems to have rankled the others, but eventually they accepted the situation as it was: CSN&Y was what Scott Young, with no attempt to avoid the obvious Canadian metaphor, calls "a loose federation." Rather than a republic. One could put it another way and say the process was everything, but that tends to suggest that mere craft overwhelmed art when some of their — his, and the group's — efforts were innovative and on occasion quite extraordinary. Industry legend insists that CSN&Y chalked up 800 hours of studio time in making DÉJÀ VU. Then there was the material that Young recorded in Britain with the London Symphony Orchestra (shades of the Stones in "*You Can't Always Get What You Want*").

Young was an irrepressible team player and yet a restless individualist. This would seem to be the essence of his career, as distinct from his music. The two forces came together in his desire to try new media and new vehicles, searching for a means that would allow him to take command of events and yet be swept up in them uncontrollably.

Consider his work in films, not just as a performer, as in *The Last Waltz* or the documentary of his *Rust Never Sleeps* tour, but in the two films he made himself, *Journey through the Past* and *Human Highway*. Each was a trial to achieve, as films usually are. He persuaded Warner to help back the former, but the company withdrew, even while going ahead with plans for the two-record soundtrack album, which thus made little sense on its own in 1972, the year before the film was released. As for *Human Highway*, the film provoked the following comment from his father: "I find it interesting that Neil can write ten songs, record them, and have the album out all within a couple of months (as he was to do in 1983 with EVERYBODY'S ROCKIN') but does not lose patience with a film, even after years of working to get it exactly as he wants it."

Consider, too, the way his tours became more and more like theatrical productions. Even in his earlier manifestation, as a comparative folkie, he evolved a stagy line of patter at the microphone, as so many performers were doing at the time. From there he naturally evolved, just as he moved inexorably towards greater technological virtuosity in the studio — so did they all, the members of that generation. The difference is that Young continued to press the purely dramatic aspect of live performance. When asked to go on the road to promote *Time Flies Away* in 1973, he envisioned a kind of slick musical rep company on the grand scale, anticipating Dylan's *Rolling Thunder Revue*. Like Dylan's, his tour featured a floating population of guest performers. Linda Ronstadt was one. In other cities he was joined by Crosby, Stills & Nash, whose presence led to speculation about a planned revival. Unlike the persistent rumour of his death at about this time, the gossip turned out eventually to be quite true.

After travelling for four years in their separate directions, CSN&Y began rehearsing together, using a 40-foot stage Young had built for that purpose at his secluded ranch an hour south of San Francisco, where one of the out buildings, according to his father's testimony, was full of stage props (his own as well as Joni Mitchell's). Later it would also contain 200,000 copies of the COMES A TIME album (1978) which he bought in order to keep off the market because he believed them to be of imperfect quality, though apparently no one else seemed able to hear the flaw. The 1974 reunion tour, culminating in a mammoth concert with Mitchell and the Band at Wembley Stadium in England, was a pronounced success, but the reunion didn't stick, and CSN&Y again separated. Young and Stills (who between them got custody of the vocal talent and the rich, rich harmonies rather than the instrumental talent) then tried their own reunion tour, but Young walked out midway through, claiming to be suffering throat problems. Suspicion has always lingered that his sore throat was the 1970s equivalent of Dylan's motorcycle accident in 1966. In any case, CSN&Y remained apart until 1989, by which time the members had endured various fates. Crosby, for example, sank deeply into drugs, alcoholism, gun-toting, and ultimately prison, as recounted all too vividly in his book *Long Time Gone*. At the other extreme, Young remade Crazy Horse in a

*"Young is genuinely
a vocalist rather than
merely a singer,
using his voice as
an instrument."*

new configuration and later formed yet another group, the Shocking Pinks. When he ventured out, as in the RUST NEVER SLEEPS tour of 1979, it was with ever more awareness of the concert as a narrative form, needing its own theatrical conventions. He recorded prolifically but stayed close to home, hobbled by his own ill health (epilepsy) and that of his son (cerebral palsy). Scott Young leaves a full, touching and unquestionably faithful picture of his son during this period.

One of Young's cruellest critics has turned out to be Marc Eliot. In his genuinely revealing book *Rockonomics: The Money behind the Music*, published in 1989, Eliot takes Young to task for hypocrisy in his protest against MTV when the station banned a Young video. The song was critical of the commercialization of rock. With respect to sincerity, Eliot likens the protest as well as the song to David Crosby's court-ordered anti-drug pronouncements. Young, he charges, is the "self-appointed integrity savior" of the rock music business. A less inflammatory interpretation, given his activities against enemies ranging from nuclear power to advertising, is that he is a concerned citizen. In either case, many Canadians remember Young most clearly in this role. The most memorable image comes in John Zaritsky's documentary *Tears Are Not Enough*, about the making of the recording of the same name, in which every imaginable star of Canadian rock, pop, and folk assembled in one studio to record a song for the benefit of Ethiopian drought victims. Viewers seem always to remember the scene in which David Foster, who was producing the record, tells Young with great diplomacy that he is a little flat. Young looks up and seems to smile. "That's my sound, man," he says.

But is it? Or if not, what is? Such questions are surprisingly difficult to answer, for on examination Young always turns out to be a far more complicated musician and composer than he at first appears. The point is worth exploring in order to show his dissimilarity to Gordon Lightfoot at the other end of the same tradition.

For all his experience both as a solo act and in groups — and it was considerable for his age — the Young who barged in on the public's awareness with Buffalo Springfield was only beginning to learn his trade. Perhaps for that reason, he was more open to experiment then than at any later period, as witness his many interesting time changes. Also, he seemed to be open to a sweeter, less brutal sound than the one he adopted later, sweeter by far than CSN&Y at their most romantic. Yet there is little or nothing in Springfield that can't be found in his mature work.

Even in the early days, he put his emphasis on vocal harmony, using

Maj7s and a lot of extended and altered chords, not just Dom7s, altered sevenths and triads. His rhythm was complicated and sophisticated and his harmony likewise, as he would frequently go out of key though playing chords on the flat 7th of the key, in the way that is typical of rock and conducive of great richness. His melodies use all sorts of non-chord tones found in classical music — that is, the melody doesn't derive from harmony the way it usually does in contemporary music. He is even fonder than Lightfoot is of suspension — hanging on to a note in chord A when moving on to chord B. He is almost baroque, in fact, in his use of *echappe*, escape notes, to embellish the melodic line. Sometimes he will clutch a stray note in a remarkable way, writing an extended chord but putting the extension in the vocal line only, not in the instrumental line. Most singers can't sing such notes in the melodic line. The difference may point to the heart of Young's talent.

His sound, man, has a lot to do with the fact that he is genuinely a vocalist rather than merely a singer, using his voice as an instrument in a way that Lightfoot, to pursue that comparison, does not. If you play connect-the-dots with his melody line, you find that you have a very jagged one indeed, with weird leaps of as much as an octave and unexpected jumps at the ends of phrases (downward jumps, usually). His phrase structure is balanced, which emphasizes the sighing quality in his voice; but he often sings at the top of his range — more like Mitchell in that respect — thus emphasizing his vocal unattractiveness, for want of a better word; at times he could almost be sending up poor Leonard Cohen, who of course can't help the way he sounds. In Young's case, one gathers, the tactic is used to get people to listen to what he says. That would also explain the way he uses what opera buffs call the recitative style — the manner of vocal discourse found in the connective passages between the arias themselves. Here his song rhythms are entirely subordinated to his speech rhythms, as in *"Trip to Tulsa"* or *"Don't Let It Get You Down."* People write that way when they wish others to understand what they're saying rather than listen to what they're doing. This gives Young a bit of common ground with Cohen, of course.

That his vocal writing was so much better than his instrumental writing is probably what made him stand out in Buffalo Springfield and so set him on his course. There is another reason which is probably even more important. Although he came of age during the folk music revival, and was at the height of his powers at the time when the folk legacy was humanizing rock 'n' roll and transforming it into the new thing called rock, Young himself, unlike all the other four artists discussed here, was more heavily indebted to rock 'n' roll than to folk. That's what makes him different. Depending on your point of view, that is also what makes him an evolutionary advance on the others.

Being like them somewhat in the shade of Dylan, who so dominated the generation in question, Young aspired to greater comfort in the folk and country traditions than he was entitled to by rights. There are scores of tiny examples, both active (the Carter-style flat-picking in "*Sea of Madness*") and passive (the way "*Cripple Creek Ferry*," a reference to the old fiddle tune "*Cripple Creek*," points up that he has much less feel for the old-time fiddle tradition than does the far funkier Robertson, for instance). One constant reminder of the difference is the use he makes of percussions: pure 1950s rock 'n' roll, not folksy foot-tapping. And then there is his harmonica playing, so superficially like Dylan's but so different on close inspection. In brief, Young has two harmonica modes. In the one, he uses the instrument like someone taking the first sip of scalding hot coffee in the morning; in the other, he uses it as a watercolourist uses a big fat No. 10 brush, to fill in the skies. It is sometimes his bass but sometimes his string section, as it were.

He is, in short, a different order of beast from the others, however broad a spectrum they themselves represent. For all that, though, he also has much in common with them. It is typical of the perverse logic of such matters that the most important piece of shared substance is likewise the most elusive and most metaphorical. It is simply that his voice runs warm at some times and hot at others but always sounds lonely. Neil Young sounds like the wind on the Prairies. There is, unfortunately, no other way to describe it.

*"Young continues
to press the purely
dramatic aspect of
live performance."*

SELECTED DISCOGRAPHIES

Compiled by Paul Stuewe

Long-play record releases are listed in order of chronological release. 'Best of' albums issued under the artist's name are included, but other anthology albums containing only one or a few tracks by the performer have been omitted. Where the artist has made guest appearances on the recordings of other musicians, a checklist of representative titles has been appended.

GORDON LIGHTFOOT

TWO TONES AT THE VILLAGE CORNER
(Chateau CLP-1012) 1962

SIDE ONE:
We Come Here to Sing
The Fox
Dark as a Dungeon
Sinnerman
This Is My Song
   (by Gordon Lightfoot)

SIDE TWO:
Kilgarry Mountain
Calypso Baby
Summer Love
Children Go Where I Send Thee
Copper Kettle
Lord I'm So Weary

(The "Two Tones" were Gordon Lightfoot and Terry Whelan)

LIGHTFOOT
(United Artists UAS-6487) 1965

SIDE ONE:
Rich Man's Spiritual
Long River
The Way I Feel
For Lovin' Me
The First Time Ever
Changes
Early Morning Rain

SIDE TWO:
Steel Rail Blues
Sixteen Miles
I'm Not Sayin'
Pride of Man
Ribbon of Darkness
Oh, Linda
Peaceful Waters

THE WAY I FEEL
(United Artists UAS-6587) 1967

SIDE ONE:
Walls
If You Got It
Softly
Crossroads
A Minor Ballad
Go Go Round

SIDE TWO:
Rosanna
Home From the Forest
I'll Be Alright
Song for a Winter's Night
Canadian Railroad Trilogy
The Way I Feel

DID SHE MENTION MY NAME
(United Artists UAS-6649) 1968

SIDE ONE:
Wherefore & Why
The Last Time I Saw Her
Black Day in July
May I
Magnificent Outpouring
Does Your Mother Know

SIDE TWO:
The Mountain and Maryann
Pussywillows, Cat-tails
I Want to Hear It from You
Something Very Special
Boss Man
Did She Mention My Name?

BACK HERE ON EARTH
(United Artists UAS-6672) 1968

SIDE ONE:
Long Way Back Home
Unsettled Ways
Long Thin Dawn
Bitter Green
The Circle Is Small
Marie Christine

SIDE TWO:
Cold Hands from New York
Affair on 8th Avenue
Don't Beat Me Down
The Gypsy
If I Could

SUNDAY CONCERT
(United Artists UAS-6714) 1969

SIDE ONE:
In a Windowpane
The Lost Children
Leaves of Grass
Medley: I'm Not Sayin',
    Ribbon of Darkness
Apology
Bitter Green

SIDE TWO:
Ballad of the Yarmouth Castle
Softly
Boss Man
Pussywillows, Cat-tails
Canadian Railroad Trilogy

SIT DOWN YOUNG STRANGER
(Reprise RS 6392) 1970

SIDE ONE:
Minstrel of the Dawn
Me and Bobby McGee
Approaching Lavender
Saturday Clothes
Cobwebs & Dust
Poor Little Allison

SIDE TWO:
Sit Down Young Stranger
If You Could Read My Mind
Baby It's Alright
Your Love's Return
The Pony Man

EARLY LIGHTFOOT
(AME 7000) 1971

SIDE ONE:
(Remember Me) I'm the One
Daisy-Doo
Adios, Adios
Is My Baby Blue Tonight
Sleep Little Jane

SIDE TWO:
Long-haired Woman
It's Too Late, He Wins
Take Care of Yourself
This is my Song
Negotiations

This album was withdrawn from release in June of 1971 after AME's rights to this material (from Lightfoot's recordings for the Chateau label) were challenged.

CLASSIC LIGHTFOOT
(United Artists UAS-5510) 1971

SIDE ONE:
The Last Time I Saw Her
Walls
Rosanna
Home from the Forest
If I Could

SIDE TWO:
Something Very Special
Long Way Back Home
Affair on 8th Avenue
Ballad of the Yarmouth Castle
Mountains and Maryann

SUMMER SIDE OF LIFE
(Reprise MS 2037) 1971

SIDE ONE:
Ten Degrees and Getting Colder
Miguel
Go My Way
Summer Side of Life
Cotton Jenny
Talking in Your Sleep

SIDE TWO:
Nous Vivons Ensemble
Same Old Loverman
Redwood Hill
Love and Maple Syrup
Cabaret

DON QUIXOTE
(Reprise MS 2056) 1972

SIDE ONE:
Don Quixote
Christian Island (Georgian Bay)
Alberta Bound
Looking at the Rain
Ordinary Man
Brave Mountaineers

SIDE TWO:
Ode to Big Blue
Second Cup of Coffee
Beautiful
On Susan's Floor
The Patriot's Dream

OLD DAN'S RECORDS
(Reprise MS 2116) 1972

SIDE ONE:
Farewell to Annabel
That Same Old Obsession
Old Dan's Records
Lazy Mornin'
You Are What I Am

SIDE TWO:
Can't Depend on Love
My Pony Won't Go
It's Worth Believin'
Mother of a Miner's Child
Hiway Songs

SUNDOWN
(Reprise MS 2177) 1973

SIDE ONE:
High and Dry
Carefree Highway
Is there Anyone Home
Somewhere in the U.S.A.
Too Late for Prayin'

SIDE TWO:
Sundown
Seven Island Suite
The List
The Watchman's Gone
Circle of Steel

FANTASTIC GORDON LIGHTFOOT
(K-TEL NC 423) 1974

RECORD ONE

SIDE ONE:
Black Day in July
Did She Mention My Name
Go Go Round
Softly
Marie Christine
Ribbon of Darkness
For Lovin' Me

SIDE TWO:
Bitter Green
If I Could
Mountain and Maryann
I'm Not Sayin'
Canadian Railroad Trilogy

RECORD TWO

SIDE ONE:
The Way I Feel
Does Your Mother Know
Steel Rail Blues
Boss Man
Cold Hands from New York
The First Time Ever

SIDE TWO:
The Last Time I Saw Her
Pussywillows, Cat-tails
Long Way Back Home
Wherefore and Why
Rosanna
Early Mornin' Rain

COLD ON THE SHOULDER
(Reprise MS 2206) 1975

SIDE ONE:
Bend in the Water
Rainy Day People
Cold on the Shoulder
The Soul Is the Rock
Bells of the Evening
Rainbow Trout

SIDE TWO:
A Tree Too Weak to Stand
All the Lovely Ladies
Fine as Fine Can Be
Cherokee Bend
Now and Then
Slide on Over

THE BEST OF GORDON LIGHTFOOT
(United Artists UAS-6754) 1975

SIDE ONE:
Go Go Round
Softly
The Way I Feel
For Lovin' Me
Early Morning Rain
I'm Not Sayin'

SIDE TWO:
Black Day in July
Did She Mention My Name
Bitter Green
Pussywillows, Cat-tails
Canadian Railroad Trilogy

A LIGHTFOOT COLLECTION
(United Artists UA-LA-189-F) 1975

SIDE ONE:
Wherefore and Why
The Gypsy
Song for a Winter's Night
Rich Man's Spiritual
Don't Beat Me Down
A Minor Ballad

SIDE TWO:
Ribbon of Darkness
Does Your Mother Know
The First Time Ever
Crossroads
Marie Christine
Steel Rail Blues

GORD'S GOLD
(Reprise 2 RX 2237) 1975

RECORD ONE

SIDE ONE:
I'm Not Sayin'/
    Ribbon of Darkness
Song for Winter's Night
Canadian Railroad Trilogy
Softly
For Lovin' Me/
    Did She Mention My Name

SIDE TWO:
Affair on 8th Avenue
Steel Rail Blues
Wherefore and Why
Bitter Green
Early Morning Rain

RECORD TWO

SIDE ONE:
Minstrel of the Dawn
Sundown
Beautiful
Summer Side of Life
Rainy Day People
Cotton Jenny

SIDE TWO:
Don Quixote
Circle of Steel
Old Dan's Record
If You Could Read My Mind
Cold on the Shoulder
Carefree Highway

THE VERY BEST OF GORDON LIGHTFOOT
(United Artists UA-LA-381E) 1975

SIDE ONE:
Early Morning Rain
I'm Not Sayin'
For Lovin' Me
The Way I Feel
Canadian Railroad Trilogy
Walls

SIDE TWO:
Did She Mention My Name
Black Day in July
Wherefore and Why
Last Time I Saw Her
Affair on 8th Avenue
If I Could

SUMMERTIME DREAM
(Reprise MS 2246) 1976

SIDE ONE:
Race among My Ruins
The Wreck of The Edmund Fitzgerald
I'm Not Supposed to Care
I'd Do It Again
Never Too Close

SIDE TWO:
Protocol
The House You Live In
Summertime Dream
Spanish Moss
Too Many Clues in This Room

ENDLESS WIRE
(Warner Brothers KBS 3149) 1978

SIDE ONE:
Daylight Katy
Sweet Guinevere
Hangdog Hotel Room
If There's a Reason
Endless Wire

SIDE TWO:
Dreamland
Songs the Minstrel Sang
Sometimes I Don't Mind
If Children Had Wings
The Circle Is Small

DREAM STREET ROSE
(Warner Brothers XHS 3429) 1980

SIDE ONE:
Sea of Tranquility
Ghosts of Cape Horn
Dream Street Rose
On the High Seas
Whisper My Name

SIDE TWO:
If You Need Me
Hey You
Make Way for the Lady
Mister Rock of Ages
The Auctioneer

SALUTE
(Warner Brothers 1-23901) 1983

SIDE ONE:
Salute (A Lot More Livin' to Do)
Gotta Get Away
Whispers of the North
Someone to Believe In
Romance

SIDE TWO:
Knotty Pine
Biscuit City
Without You
Tattoo
Broken Dreams

EAST OF MIDNIGHT
(Warner Brothers 25482) 1986

SIDE ONE:
Stay Loose
Morning Glory
East of Midnight
A Lesson in Love
Anything for Love

SIDE TWO:
Let It Ride
Ecstasy Made Easy
You Just Gotta Be
A Passing Ship
I'll Tag Along

GORD'S GOLD VOLUME II
(Warner Brothers) 1988

SIDE ONE:
If It Should Please You
Endless Wire
Hangdog Hotel Room
I'm Not Supposed to Care
High and Dry
The Wreck of the Edmund Fitzgerald
The Pony Man

SIDE TWO:
Make Way (For the Lady)
Race among the Ruins
Christian Island
All the Lovely Ladies
Alberta Bound
Cherokee Bend
Triangle
Shadows
Baby Step Back

LEONARD COHEN

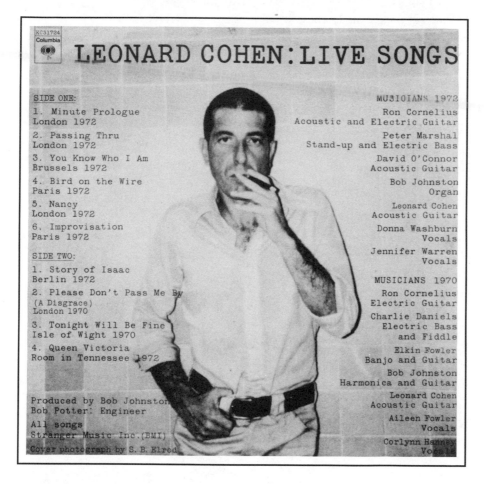

KC31724
Columbia

LEONARD COHEN: LIVE SONGS

SIDE ONE:

1. Minute Prologue
London 1972

2. Passing Thru
London 1972

3. You Know Who I Am
Brussels 1972

4. Bird on the Wire
Paris 1972

5. Nancy
London 1972

6. Improvisation
Paris 1972

SIDE TWO:

1. Story of Isaac
Berlin 1972

2. Please Don't Pass Me By
(A Disgrace)
London 1970

3. Tonight Will Be Fine
Isle of Wight 1970

4. Queen Victoria
Room in Tennessee 1972

Produced by Bob Johnston
Bob Potter: Engineer
All songs
Stranger Music Inc.(BMI)
Cover photograph by S. B. Elrod

MUSICIANS 1972

Ron Cornelius
Acoustic and Electric Guitar

Peter Marshal
Stand-up and Electric Bass

David O'Connor
Acoustic Guitar

Bob Johnston
Organ

Leonard Cohen
Acoustic Guitar

Donna Washburn
Vocals

Jennifer Warren
Vocals

MUSICIANS 1970

Ron Cornelius
Electric Guitar

Charlie Daniels
Electric Bass
and Fiddle

Elkin Fowler
Banjo and Guitar

Bob Johnston
Harmonica and Guitar

Leonard Cohen
Acoustic Guitar

Aileen Fowler
Vocals

Corlynn Hanney
Vocals

SONGS OF LEONARD COHEN
(Columbia CS 9533) 1968

SIDE ONE:
Suzanne
Master Song
Winter Lady
The Stranger Song
Sisters of Mercy

SIDE TWO:
So Long, Marianne
Hey, That's No Way to Say Goodbye
Stories of the Street
Teachers
One of Us Cannot Be Wrong

SONGS FROM A ROOM
(Columbia CS 9767) 1969

SIDE ONE:
Bird on the Wire
Story of Issac
A Bunch of Lonesome Heroes
The Partisan
Seems So Long Ago, Nancy

SIDE TWO:
The Old Revolution
The Butcher
You Know Who I Am
Lady Midnight
Tonight Will Be Fine

SONGS OF LOVE AND HATE
(Columbia KC 30103) 1971

SIDE ONE:
Love Calls You by Your Name
Dress Rehearsal Rag
Avalanche
Last Year's Man

SIDE TWO:
Diamonds in the Mind
Sing Another Song, Boys
Joan of Arc
Famous Blue Raincoat

LIVE SONGS
(Columbia KC 31724) 1973

SIDE ONE:
Minute Prologue
Passing Thru
You Know Who I Am
Bird on the Wire
Nancy
Improvisation

SIDE TWO:
Story of Isaac
Please Don't Pass Me By
Tonight Will Be Fine
Queen Victoria

NEW SKIN FROM THE OLD CEREMONY
(Columbia KC 33167) 1974

SIDE ONE:
Is This What You Wanted
Chelsea Hotel #2
Lover Lover Lover
Field Commander Cohen
Why Don't You Try

SIDE TWO:
There Is a War
A Singer Must Die
I Tried to Leave You
Who by Fire
Take this Longing
Leaving Greensleeves

THE BEST OF LEONARD COHEN
(Columbia KES 90334) 1976

SIDE ONE:
Suzanne
Sisters of Mercy
So Long, Marianne
Lady Midnight
The Partisan
Bird on the Wire

SIDE TWO:
Hey, That's No Way to Say Goodbye
Famous Blue Raincoat
Last Year's Man
Chelsea Hotel
Who by Fire
Take this Longing

DEATH OF A LADIES' MAN
(Columbia KC 3125) 1977

SIDE ONE:
True Love Leaves No Traces
Iodine
Paper-thin Hotel
Memories

SIDE TWO:
I Left a Woman Waiting
Don't Go Home with You Hard-on
Fingerprints
Death of a Ladies' Man

RECENT SONGS
(Columbia KC 36364) 1979

SIDE ONE:
The Guests
Humbled in Love
The Window
Came So Far for Beauty
The Lost Canadian

SIDE TWO:
The Traitor
Our Land of Solitude
The Gypsy's Wife
The Smokey Life
Ballad of the Absent Mare

VARIOUS POSITIONS
(Passport PB 6045) 1985

SIDE ONE:
Dance Me to the End of Love
Coming Back to You
The Law
The Night Comes On
Hallelujah

SIDE TWO:
The Captain
Hunter's Lullaby
Heart With No Companion
If It Be Your Will

I'M YOUR MAN
(Columbia FC 44191) 1988

SIDE ONE:
First We Take Manhattan
Ain't No Cure for Love
Everybody Knows
I'm Your Man
Take This Waltz

SIDE TWO:
Jazz Police
I Can't Forget
Tower of Song

Leonard Cohen appears as a guest artist on Earl Scrugg's ANNIVERSARY SPECIAL (Columbia KC 33416) and on Jennifer Warnes' FAMOUS BLUE RAINCOAT (Attic 1227).

JONI MITCHELL

JONI MITCHELL
(Reprise RS 6293) 1968

SIDE ONE:
I Had a King
Michael from Mountains
Night in the City
Marcie
Nathan La Franeer

SIDE TWO:
Sistowbell Lane
Dawntreader
Pirate of Penance
Song to a Seagull
Cactus Tree

CLOUDS
(Reprise RS 6341) 1969

SIDE ONE:
Tin Angel
Chelsea Morning
I Don't Know Where I Stand
That Song about the Midway
Roses Blue

SIDE TWO:
The Gallery
I Think I Understand
Songs to Aging Children Gone
The Fiddle and the Drum
Both Sides Now

LADIES OF THE CANYON
(Reprise RS 6376) 1970

SIDE ONE:
Morning Morgantown
For Free
Conversation
Ladies of the Canyon
Willy
The Arrangement

SIDE TWO:
Rainy Night House
The Priest
Blue Boy
Big Yellow Taxi
Woodstock
The Circle Game

BLUE
(Reprise MS 2038) 1971

SIDE ONE:
All I Want
My Old Man
Little Green
Carey
Blue

SIDE TWO:
California
This Flight Tonight
River
A Case of You
The Last Time I Saw Richard

FOR THE ROSES
(Asylum SD 5057) 1972

SIDE ONE:
Banquet
Cold Blue Steel and Sweet Fire
Baranghill
Lesson in Survival
Let the Wind Carry Me
For the Roses

SIDE TWO:
See You Sometime
Electricity
You Turn Me On, I'm a Radio
Blond in the Bleachers
Woman of Heart and Mind
Judgement of the Moon and
the Stars (Ludwig's Tune)

COURT AND SPARK
(Asylum 7ES-1001) 1974

SIDE ONE:
Court and Spark
Help Me
Free Man in Paris
People's Parties
Some Situation

SIDE TWO:
Car on a Hill
Down to You
Just Like This Train
Raised on Robbery
Trouble Child
Twisted

MILES OF AISLES
(Asylum AB-202) 1974

SIDE ONE:
You Turn Me On, I'm a Radio
Big Yellow Taxi
Rainy Night House
Woodstock

SIDE TWO:
Cactus Tree
Cold Blue Steel & Sweet Fire
Woman of Heart and Mind
A Case of You
Blue

SIDE THREE:
Circle Game
People's Parties
All I Want
Real Food for Free
Both Sides Now

SIDE FOUR:
Carey
The Last Time I Saw Richard
Jericho
Love or Money

THE HISSING OF SUMMER LAWNS
(Asylum 7ES-1051) 1975

SIDE ONE:
In France They Kiss on
    Main Street
The Jungle Line
Edith and the Kingpin
Don't Interrupt the Sorrow
Shades of Scarlet Conquering

SIDE TWO:
The Hissing of Summer Lawns
The Boho Dance
Harry's House/Centerpiece
Sweet Bird
Shadows and Light

HEJIRA
(Asylum 7ES-1087) 1976

SIDE ONE:
Coyote
Amelia
Furry Sings the Blues
A Strange Boy
Hejira

SIDE TWO:
Song for Sharon
Black Crow
Blue Motel Room
Refuge of the Roads

DON JUAN'S RECKLESS DAUGHTER
(Asylum 701) 1977

SIDE ONE:
Overture — Cotton Avenue
Talk to Me
Jericho
Paprika Plains
Otis and Marlena
The Tenth World

SIDE TWO:
Dreamland
Don Juan's Reckless Daughter
Off Night Backstreet
The Silky Veils of Ardour

MINGUS
(Elektra 5E-505) 1979

SIDE ONE:
Happy Birthday 1975 (RAP)
God Must Be a Boogie Man
Funeral (RAP)
A Chair in the Sky
The Wolf That Lives in Lindsey
I's a Muggin' (RAP)

SIDE TWO:
Sweet Sucker Dance
Coin in the Pocket
The Dry Cleaner from Des Moines
Lucky (RAP)
Goodbye Pork Pie Hat

SHADOWS AND LIGHT
(Asylum 2XBB-704) 1980

SIDE ONE:
Intro
In France They Kiss
    on Main Street
Edith and the Kingpin
Coyote
Goodbye Pork Pie Hat

SIDE TWO:
The Dry Cleaner from Des Moines
Amelia
Pat's Solo
Hejira

SIDE THREE:
Black Crew
Don's Solo
Dreamland
Free Man in Paris
Band Intro.
Furry Sings the Blues

SIDE FOUR:
Why Do Fool's Fall in Love
Shadows and Light
God Must Be a Boogie Man
Woodstock

WILD THINGS RUN FAST
(Geffen GHS 2019) 1982

SIDE ONE:
Chinese Café
Unchained Melody
Wild Things Run Fast
Ladies Man
Solid Love
Moon at the Window
Underneath the Streetlight

SIDE TWO:
Be Cool
(You're So Square) Baby I Don't Care
You Dream Flat Tires
Man to Man
Love

DOG EAT DOG
(Geffen GHS 24074) 1985

SIDE ONE:
Good Friends
Fiction
The Three Great Stimulants
Tax Free
Smokin' (Empty, Try Another)

SIDE TWO:
Dog Eat Dog
Shiny Toys
Ethiopia
Impossible Dream
Lucky Girl

CHALK MARKS IN A RAIN STORM
1988

SIDE ONE:
My Secret Palace
Number One
Lakota
The Tea Leaf Prophecy
    (Lay Down Your Arms)
Dancin' Clown

SIDE TWO:
Cool Water
The Beat of Black Wings
Snakes and Ladders
The Reoccuring Dream
A Bird That Whistles

Joni Mitchell appears as a guest artist on:

Eric Anderson's BLUE RIVER (Columbia KC 31062) and BE TRUE TO YOU (Artists 4033)
Graham Nash's WILD TALES (Atlantic SD 7288)
David Crosby's IF I COULD ONLY REMEMBER MY NAME (Atlantic K 40320)
James Taylor's SWEET BABY JAMES (Warner Brothers BS 1843) and MUD SLIDE SLIM AND THE BLUE HORIZON (Warner Brothers BS 2561)
Joan Baez's GRACIAS A LA VIDA (HERE'S TO LIFE) (A & M 63614) and DIAMONDS AND RUST (A & M 64527)
The Band's THE LAST WALTZ (Warner Brothers 3WS 3145)
David Blue's COMIN' BACK FOR MORE (Asylum 7ES-1043)
Jimmy Webb's LETTERS (Reprise RS 2055) and LANDS END (Asylum SC 5070)
Simon and Marijke's SON OF AMERICA (A & M SP 4309)
L.A. Express's SHADOW PLAY (Caribou 34355)
Paul Horn's VISIONS (Epic 32837)
Jackson Browne's FOR EVERYMAN (Asylum 5067)

ROBBIE ROBERTSON

"MR. DYNAMO"
(Roulette R 25102) 1960

SIDE ONE:
Clara
Hey Boba Lou
Dreams Do Come True
Hay Ride
Honey Don't

SIDE TWO:
Lonely Hours
Sick and Tired
Love Me Like You Can
You Cheated, You Lied
Baby Jean
Southern Love

On this album, Ronnie Hawkins — vocals and guitar, Robbie Robertson and Jimmy Ray Paulman — guitar, Will "Pop" Jones — piano, James G. Evans — bass, and Levon Helm — drums.

THE BEST OF RONNIE HAWKINS
(Roulette R 25255) 1962

SIDE ONE:	*SIDE TWO:*
Bo Diddley	Who Do You Love
Come Love	I Feel Good
Honey Love	Searching
High Blood Pressure	Mojo Man
Arkansas	Sexy Ways
Bossman	You Know I Love You

On this and the following album Hawkins was accompanied by the future members of the Band: Robbie Robertson — guitar, Levon Helm — drums, Rick Danko — bass, and Garth Hudson — organ and saxophone, and Richard Manuel — piano.

MOJO MAN
(Roulette R 25390) 1964

SIDE ONE:	*SIDE TWO:*
Matchbox	Ballad of Caryl Chessman
Lonely Hours	Suzie-Q
Summertime	Southern Love
One Out of a Hundred	Your Cheatin' Heart
Further On Up the Road	She's 19 (incorrectly identified as "What a Party" on the jacket and disc label)

THE BEST OF RONNIE HAWKINS FEATURING HIS BAND
(Roulette R 42045) 1965

SIDE ONE:	*SIDE TWO:*
Ruby Baby	Mojo Man
Odessa	Baby Jean
The Death of Floyd Collins	The Ballad of Caryl Chessman
Clara	Who Do You Love
Bo Diddley	Mary Lou

This is a compilation album from various Hawkins groups.

MUSIC FROM BIG PINK
(Capitol SKAO 2955) 1968

SIDE ONE:
Tears of Rage
To Kingdom Come
In a Station
Caledonia Mission
The Weight

SIDE TWO:
We Can Talk
Long Black Veil
Chest Fever
Lonesome Suzie
This Wheel's on Fire
I Shall Be Released

Robbie Robertson — vocals and guitar, Richard Manuel — vocals and piano, Garth Hudson — organ and saxophone, Rick Danko — vocals and bass, and Levon Helm — drums.

THE BAND
(Capitol STAO 132) 1969

SIDE ONE:
Across the Great Divide
Rag Mama Rag
The Night They Drove
    Old Dixie Down
When You Awake
Up on Cripple Creek
Whispering Pines

SIDE TWO:
Jemima Surrender
Rockin' Chair
Look Out Cleveland
Jawbone
The Unfaithful Servant
King Harvest (Has Surely Come)

STAGE FRIGHT
(Capitol SW 425) 1970

SIDE ONE:
Strawberry Wine
Sleeping
Time to Kill
Just Another Whistle Stop
All La Glory

SIDE TWO:
The Shape I'm In
The W.S. Walcott Medicine Show
Daniel and the Sacred Harp
Stage Fright
The Rumor

CAHOOTS
(Capitol SMAS 651) 1971

SIDE ONE:
Life Is a Carnival
When I Paint My Masterpiece
Last of the Blacksmiths
Where Do We Go from Here?
4% Pantomime

SIDE TWO:
Shoot-out in Chinatown
The Moon Struck One
Thinkin' Out Loud
Smoke Signal
Volcano
The River Hymn

ROCK OF AGES
(Capitol SABB 11045) 1972

SIDE ONE:
Don't Do It
King Harvest (Has Surely Come)
Caledonia Mission
Get Up Jake
W.S. Walcott Medicine Show

SIDE TWO:
Stage Fright
The Night They Drove Old Dixie Down
Rag Mama Rag

SIDE THREE:
The Weight
The Shape I'm In
Unfaithful Servant
Life Is a Carnival

SIDE FOUR:
The Genetic Method
Chest Fever
(I Don't Want to) Hang Up My Rock
    and Roll Shoes

MOONDOG MATINEE
(Capitol SW 11214) November 1973

SIDE ONE:
Ain't Got No Home
Holy Cow
Share Your Love
Mystery Train
Third Man Theme

SIDE TWO:
Promised Land
The Great Pretender
I'm Ready
Saved
A Change Is Gonna Come

PLANET WAVES
(Asylum 7E-1003) Bob Dylan and The Band 1974

SIDE ONE:
On a Night Like This
Going Going Gone
Tough Mama
Hazel
Something There Is About You

SIDE TWO:
Forever Young
Dirge
You Angel You
Never Say Goodbye
Wedding Song

BEFORE THE FLOOD
(Asylum AB 201) Bob Dylan and The Band 1974

SIDE ONE:
Most Likely You Go Your Way
    (and I'll Go Mine)
Lay Lady Lay
Rainy Day Women #12 and 35
Knockin' on Heaven's Door
It Ain't Me, Babe
Ballad of a Thin Man

SIDE TWO:
Up on Cripple Creek
I Shall Be Released
Endless Highway
The Night They Drove Old Dixie Down
Stage Fright

SIDE THREE:
Don't Think Twice, It's All Right
Just Like a Woman
It's Alright Ma (I'm Only Bleeding)
The Shape I'm In
When You Awake

SIDE FOUR:
All along the Watchtower
Highway 61 Revisited
Like a Rolling Stone
Blowin' in the Wind

THE BASEMENT TAPES
(Columbia C2X 33682) Bob Dylan and the Band 1975

SIDE ONE:
Odds and Ends
Orange Juice Blues
    (Blues for Breakfast)
Million Dollar Bash
Yazoo Street Scandal
Goin' to Acapulco
Katie's Been Gone

SIDE TWO:
Lo and Behold
Bessie Smith
Clothesline Saga
Applesucking Tree
Please, Mrs. Henry
Tears of Rage

SIDE THREE
Too Much of Nothing
Yea! Heavy and a Bottle of Bread
Ain't No More Cane
Crash on the Levee
    (Down in the Flood)
Ruben Demus
Tiny Montgomery

SIDE FOUR:
You Ain't Goin' Nowhere
Don't Ya Tell Henry
Nothing Was Delivered
Open the Door, Homer
Long Distance Operator
This Wheel's on Fire

NORTHERN LIGHTS — SOUTHERN CROSS
(Capitol ST 11440) 1975

SIDE ONE:
Forbidden Fruit
Hobo Jungle
Ophelia
Acadian Driftwood

SIDE TWO:
Ring Your Bell
It Makes No Difference
Jupiter Hollow
Rags and Bones

BEST OF THE BAND
(Capitol ST 11553) 1976

SIDE ONE:
Up on Cripple Creek
The Shape I'm In
The Weight
It Makes No Difference
Life Is a Carnival

SIDE TWO:
Twilight
Don't Do It
Tears of Rage
Stage Fright
Ophelia
The Night They Drove Old Dixie Down

ISLANDS
(Capitol SW 11602) 1977

SIDE ONE:
Street Walker
The Islands
Right as Rain
Ain't That a Lot of Love
This Must Be Christmas

SIDE TWO:
Let the Night Fall
Pepote Range
Georgia on My Mind
Knockin' Lost John
Livin' in a Dream

THE LAST WALTZ
(Warner Brothers 3WS 3146) 1978

SIDE ONE:
The Last Waltz
Up on Cripple Creek
Who Do You Love
Helpless
Stage Fright

SIDE TWO:
Coyote
Dry Your Eyes
It Makes No Difference
Such a Night

SIDE THREE:
The Night They Drove
    Old Dixie Down
Mystery Train
Mannish Boy
Farther on up the Road

SIDE FOUR:
The Shape I'm In
Down South in New Orleans
Ophelia
Tura Lura Lura (That's an Irish Lullaby)
Caravan

SIDE FIVE:
Life is a Carnival
Baby Let Me Follow You Down
I Don't Believe You (She Acts Like
    We Never Have Met)
Forever Young
Baby Let Me Follow You
    Down (reprise)
I Shall Be Released

SIDE SIX:
The Last Waltz Suite:
    The Well/Evangeline/Out of the Blue/
    The Weight/The Last Waltz Refrain/
    The Theme from the Last Waltz

ANTHOLOGY
(Capitol SKBO 11856) 1978

SIDE ONE:
The Weight
Chest Fever
I Shall Be Released
Rag Mama Rag
The Night They Drove Old
    Dixie Down

SIDE TWO:
Up on Cripple Creek
King Harvest (Has Surely Come)
Stage Fright
The Shape I'm In
Daniel and the Sacred Harp

ROBBIE ROBERTSON
(Geffen GHS 24160) 1988

SIDE ONE:
Fallen Angel
Showdown at Big Sky
Broken Arrow
Sweet Fire of Love

SIDE TWO:
American Roulette
Somewhere Down the Crazy River
Hell's Half Acre
Sorry, Got Caught in the Moonlight
Testimony

Robbie Robertson appears as a guest artist on:

Jessie Winchester's JESSE WINCHESTER (Ampex A-10104)
Neil Diamond's BEAUTIFUL NOISE (Columbia PC 33965)
Libby Titus's LIBBY TITUS (Columbia PC 34152)
John Hammond's I CAN TELL (Atlantic SC 8152), SO MANY ROADS (Vanguard VSD 79198) and MIRRORS (Vanguard VSD 79245)
Bob Dylan's BLONDE ON BLONDE (Columbia C2S 841) and SELF PORTRAIT (Columbia C2X 30050)
Ringo Starr's RINGO (Apple SWAL 3413) and GOODNIGHT VIENNA (Apple SWAL 3417)
Joni Mitchell's COURT AND SPARK (Asylum 7ES-1001)
Carly Simon's HOTCAKES (Elektra 7E-1002
Jackie Lomax's THREE (Warner Brothers BS 2591)
Levon Helm's LEVON HELM AND THE RCO ALL STARS (ABC 1017)
Rick Danko's RICK DANKO (Arista 4141)

NEIL YOUNG

BUFFALO SPRINGFIELD
(ATCO SD-33-200) 1966

SIDE ONE:

For What It's Worth
Go and Say Goodbye
Sit Down I Think I Love You
Nowadays Clancy Can't Even Sing
Hot Dusty Roads
Everybody's Wrong

SIDE TWO:

Flying on the Ground Is Wrong
Burned
Do I Have to Come Right Out and Say It
Leave
Out of My Mind
Pay the Price

This and the next three albums record Young's career with the Buffalo Springfield, which originally consisted of himself, Steven Stills and Richie Furay — vocals and guitar, Dewey Martin — vocals and drums, and Bruce Palmer — bass. Midway through the recording of THE LAST TIME AROUND Palmer left the band and Jim Messina — vocals and bass, Jim Fielder — bass, and Doug Hastings — guitar, joined for a short period of time before the group disbanded.

BUFFALO SPRINGFIELD AGAIN
(ATCO SD-33-226) 1967

SIDE ONE:
Mr. Soul
A Child's Claim to Fame
Everydays
Expecting to Fly
Bluebird

SIDE TWO:
Hung Upside Down
Sad Memory
Good Time Boy
Rock & Roll
Broken Arrow

LAST TIME AROUND
(ATCO SD-33-256) 1968

SIDE ONE:
Uno Mundo
On the Way Home
It's So Hard to Wait
Pretty Girl Why
Four Days Gone
Carefree Country Day

SIDE TWO:
Special Care
Hour of Not Quite Rain
Questions
I Am a Child
Merry-Go-Round
Kind Woman

RETROSPECTIVE: THE BEST OF THE BUFFALO SPRINGFIELD
(ATCO SD-33-283)

SIDE ONE:
For What It's Worth
Mr. Soul
Sit Down I Think I Love You
Kind Woman
Bluebird
On the Way Home

SIDE TWO:
Nowadays Clancy Can't Even Sing
Broken Arrow
Rock & Roll Woman
I Am a Child
Go and Say Goodbye
Expecting to Fly

NEIL YOUNG
(Reprise RS 6317) 1969

SIDE ONE:
Emperor of Wyoming
The Loner
If I Could Have Her Tonight
I've Been Waiting for You
The Old Laughing Lady

SIDE TWO:
String Quartet from Whiskey Boot Hill
Here We Are in the Years
What Did You Do to My Life
I've Loved Her So Long
The Last Trip to Tulsa

EVERYBODY KNOWS THIS IS NOWHERE
(Reprise RS 6349) Neil Young with Crazy Horse 1969

SIDE ONE:
Cinnamon Girl
Everybody Knows This Is Nowhere
Round and Round (It Won't Be Long)
Down by the River

SIDE TWO:
This Losing End (When You're On)
Running Day (Requiem for the Rockets)
Cowgirl in the Sand

Crazy Horse is basically Young's backup group, although they have recorded three albums on their own. Billy Talbot — bass and Ralph Molina — drums have been members since its inception, and at various times George Whitsell, Nils Lofgren, Greg Leroy and Frank Sampedro, guitar, John Blanton — keyboards, and the late Danny Whitten (to whom TONIGHT'S THE NIGHT is dedicated) — vocals and guitar, have played with the band.

DÉJÀ VU
(Atlantic SD 7200) Crosby, Stills, Nash and Young 1970

SIDE ONE:
Carry On
Teach Your Children
Almost Cut My Hair
Helpless
Woodstock

SIDE TWO:
Déjà Vu
Our House
4:20
Country Girl
Everybody I Love You

CSN&Y consists of Young, David Crosby and Graham Nash — vocals and guitar, and Stephen Stills — vocals, guitar, bass and keyboards, performing alone or in various combinations with rhythm accompaniment (initially Greg Reeves — bass, and Dallas Taylor — drums, and later Calvin Samuels — bass, and Johnny Barbata — drums).

AFTER THE GOLD RUSH
(Reprise RS 6383) 1970

SIDE ONE:
Tell Me Why
After the Gold Rush
Only Love Can Break Your Heart
Southern Man
Till the Morning Comes

SIDE TWO:
Oh, Lonesome Me
Don't Let It Bring You Down
Birds
When You Dance I Can Really Love
I Believe in You
Cripple Creek Ferry

4-WAY STREET
(Atlantic SD 2-902) Crosby, Stills, Nash and Young 1971

RECORD ONE

SIDE ONE:
Suite, Judy Blue Eyes
On the Way Home
Teach Your Children
Triad
The Lee Shore
Chicago

SIDE TWO:
Right Between the Eyes
Cowgirl in the Sand
Don't Let It Bring You Down
49 Bye Byes/America's Children
Love the One You're With

RECORD TWO

SIDE ONE:
Pre-Road Downs
Long Time Gone
Southern Man

SIDE TWO:
Ohio
Carry On
Find the Cost of Freedom

HARVEST
(Reprise MS 2032) 1972

SIDE ONE:
Out on the Weekend
Harvest
A Man Needs a Maid
Heart of Gold
Are You Ready for the Country

SIDE TWO:
Old Man
There's a World
Alabama
The Needle and the Damage Done
Words (Between the Lines of Age)

A JOURNEY THROUGH THE PAST
(Reprise 2XS 6840) 1972

SIDE ONE:
For What It's Worth/Mr. Soul
Rock and Roll Woman
Find the Cost of Freedom
Ohio

SIDE TWO:
Southern Man
Are You Ready for the Country
Let Me Call You Sweetheart
Alabama

SIDE THREE:
Words

SIDE FOUR:
Relativity
Invitation
The "King of Kings" Theme
Soldier
Let's Go Away for a While

TIME FADES AWAY
(Reprise MS 2151) 1973

SIDE ONE:
Time Fades Away
Journey through the Past
Yonder Stands the Sinner
L.A.
Love in Mind

SIDE TWO:
Don't Be Denied
The Bridge
Last Dance

BUFFALO SPRINGFIELD
(ATCO 2Sa-806) 1973

RECORD ONE

SIDE ONE:
For What It's Worth
Sit Down I Think I Love You
Nowadays Clancy Can't Even Sing
Go and Say Goodbye
Pay the Price
Burned
Out of My Mind

SIDE TWO:
Mr. Soul
Bluebird
Broken Arrow
Rock & Roll Woman

RECORD TWO

SIDE ONE:
Expecting to Fly
Hung Upside Down
A Child's Claim to Fame
On the Way Home
I Am a Child

SIDE TWO:
Pretty Girl Why
Special Care
Uno Mundo
In the Hour of Not Quite Rain
Four Days Gone
Questions

ON THE BEACH
(Warner Brothers R 2180) 1974

SIDE ONE:
Walk On
See the Sky about to Rain
Revolution Blues
For the Turnstiles
Vampire Blues

SIDE TWO:
On the Beach
Motion Pictures
Ambulance Blues

SO FAR
(Atlantic SD 18100) Crosby, Stills, Nash and Young 1974

SIDE ONE:
Déjà Vu
Helplessly Hoping
Wooden Ships
Teach Your Children
Ohio
Find the Cost of Freedom

SIDE TWO:
Woodstock
Our House
Helpless
Guinnevere
Suite: Judy Blue Eyes

TONIGHT'S THE NIGHT
(Reprise MS 2221) 1975

SIDE ONE:
Tonight's the Night
Speakin' Out
World on a String
Borrowed Tune
Come on Baby Let's Go Downtown

SIDE TWO:
Roll Another Number (For the Road)
Albuquerque
New Mama
Lookout Joe
Tired Eyes
Tonight's the Night — Part II

ZUMA
(Warner Brothers MS 2242) Neil Young with Crazy Horse 1975

SIDE ONE:
Don't Cry No Tears
Danger Bird
Pardon My Heart
Lookin' for a Love
Barstool Blues

SIDE TWO:
Stupid Girl
Drive Back
Cortez the Killer
Through My Sails

LONG MAY YOU RUN
(Warner Brothers MS 2253) The Stills-Young Band 1976

SIDE ONE:
Long May You Run
Make Love to You
Midnight on the Bay
Black Coral
Ocean Girl

SIDE TWO:
Let It Shine
12/8 Blues
Fontainebleau
Guardian Angel

DECADE
(Reprise 3RS 2257) 1976

SIDE ONE:
Down to the Wire
Burned
Mr. Soul
Broken Arrow
Expecting to Fly
Sugar Mountain

SIDE TWO:
I Am a Child
The Lonely
The Old Laughing Lady
Cinnamon Girl
Down by the River

SIDE THREE
Cowgirl in the Sand
I Believe in You
After the Gold Rush
Southern Man
Helpless

SIDE FOUR:
Ohio
Soldier
Old Man
A Man Needs a Maid
Harvest
Heart of Gold
Star of Bethlehem

SIDE FIVE:
The Needle and the Damage Done
Tonight's the Night
Tired Eyes
Walk On
For the Turnstiles
Winterlong
Deep Forbidden Lake

SIDE SIX:
Like a Hurricane
Love Is a Rose
Cortez the Killer
Campaigner
Long May You Run

AMERICAN STARS'N BARS
(Reprise KMS 2261) 1977

SIDE ONE:
The Old Country Waltz
Saddle Up the Palomino
Hey Babe
Hold Back the Tears
Bite the Bullet

SIDE TWO:
Star of Bethlehem
Will to Love
Like a Hurricane
Homegrown

COMES A TIME
(Reprise RS 2266) 1978

SIDE ONE:
Goin' Back
Comes a Time
Look Out for My Love
Lotta Love
Piece of Mind

SIDE TWO:
Human Highway
Already One
Field of Opportunity
Motorcycle Mama
Four Strong Winds

RUST NEVER SLEEPS
(Reprise RS 2295) 1979

SIDE ONE:
My My, Hey Hey (Out of the Blue)
Thrasher
Ride My Llama
Pocahontas
Sail Away

SIDE TWO:
Powderfinger
Welfare Mother
Sedan Delivery
Hey Hey, My My (Into the Black)

LIVE RUST
(Reprise RS 2296) 1979

SIDE ONE:
Sugar Mountain
I'm a Child
Comes a Time
After the Gold Rush
My My, Hey Hey (Out of the Blue)
When You Dance I Can Really Love
The Lover/The Needle and the
    Damage Done/Lotta Love/Sedan
    Delivery/Powderfinger

SIDE TWO:
Cortez the Killer
Cinnamon Girl
Like a Hurricane

Hey Hey, My My (Into the Black)
Tonight's the Night

HAWKS AND DOVES
(Reprise RS 2297) 1980

SIDE ONE:
Little Wing
The Old Homestead
Lost in Space
Captain Kennedy

SIDE TWO:
Stayin' Power
Coastline
Union Man
Comin' Apart at Every Nail
Hawks and Doves

REACTOR
(Reprise RS 2304) 1981

SIDE ONE:
Opera Star
Surfer Joe and Mac the Sleaze
T-Bone
Get Back on It

SIDE TWO:
Southern Pacific
Motor City
Rapid Transit
Shots

TRANS
(Geffen GHS 2018) 1983

SIDE ONE:
Little Thing Called Love
Computer Age
We Run Control
Transformer Man
Computer Cowboy (a.k.a. Skycrusher)

SIDE TWO:
Hold on to Your Love
Sample and Hold
Mr. Soul
Like an Inca

NEIL YOUNG AND THE SHOCKING PINKS
(Geffen GHS 4013) 1983

SIDE ONE:
Betty Lou's Got a
    New Pair of Shoes
Rainin' in My Heart
Payola Blues
Wonderin'
Kinda Fonda Wanda

SIDE TWO:
Jellyroll Man
Bright Lights, Big City
Cry, Cry, Cry
Mystery Train
Everybody's Rockin'

OLD WAYS
(Geffen GHS 24068) 1985

SIDE ONE:
The Wayward Wind
Get Back to the Country
Are There Any More
    Real Cowboys?
Misfits

SIDE TWO:
California Sunset
Old Ways
My Boy
Bound for Glory
Where Is the Highway Tonight?

LANDING ON WATER
(Geffen GHS 24109) 1986

SIDE ONE:
Weight of the World
Violent Side
Hippie Dream
Bad News Beast
Touch the Night

SIDE TWO:
People on the Street
Hard Luck Stories
I Got a Problem
Pressure
Drifter

LIFE
(Geffen GHS 24154) 1987

SIDE ONE:
Mideast Vacation
Long Walk Home
Around the World
Inca Queen

SIDE TWO:
Too Lonely
Prisoners of Rock'n'Roll
Cryin' Eyes
When Your Lonely Heart Break
We Never Danceds

THIS NOTE'S FOR YOU
(Reprise RS 25719) 1988

SIDE ONE:
Ten Men Workin'
This Note's For You
Coupe de Ville
Life in the City
Twilight

SIDE TWO:
Married Man
Sunny Insider
Can't Believe Your Lyin'
Hey Hey
One Thing

Neil Young appears as a guest artist on:

Nils Lofgren's GRIN (Spindizzy Z 30321)
Joni Mitchell's HEJIRA (Asylum 7ES-1087)
Crazy Horse's CRAZY MOON (RCA AFLI 3054)
The Band's THE LAST WALTZ (Warner Brothers 3WS 3146)